The Music
Library

The History
of Latin Music

*The Music
Library*

The History
of Latin Music

Other books in this series include:

The History of Gospel Music
The History of Punk Rock
The History of Rap and Hip-Hop
The History of Reggae
The History of the Blues
The History of World Music

The Music
Library

The History
of Latin Music

By Stuart A. Kallen

LUCENT BOOKS

An imprint of Thomson Gale, a part of The Thomson Corporation

Detroit • New York • San Francisco • San Diego • New Haven, Conn. • Waterville, Maine • London • Munich

LIBRARY OF CONGRESS CATALOGING-IN-PUBLICATION DATA

Kallen, Stuart A., 1955–
    The history of Latin Music / by Stuart A. Kallen.
        p. cm. — (The music library)
    Includes bibliographical references and index.
        ISBN 1-59018-737-7 (hard cover : alk. paper) 1. Music—Latin America—History
and criticism—Juvenile literature. I. Title. II. Series: Music library (San Diego, Calif.)
ML199.K35 2006
780.98—dc22
                                                                2006004676

Printed in the United States of America

• Contents •

Foreword   8
Introduction: A Global Beat   10

Chapter One
Roots Music   14

Chapter Two
Caribbean Spice   30

Chapter Three
Brazilian Beats   45

Chapter Four
Music of South America   62

Chapter Five
Mexican Music in Two Nations   77

Notes   93
For Further Reading   95
Index   97
Picture Credits   104
About the Author   104

• Foreword •

In the nineteenth century, English novelist Charles Kingsley wrote, "Music speaks straight to our hearts and spirits, to the very core and root of our souls. . . . Music soothes us, stirs us up . . . melts us to tears." As Kingsley stated, music is much more than just a pleasant arrangement of sounds. It is the resonance of emotion, a joyful noise, a human endeavor that can soothe the spirit or excite the soul. Musicians can also imitate the expressive palate of the earth, from the violent fury of a hurricane to the gentle flow of a babbling brook.

The word *music* is derived from the fabled Greek muses, the children of Apollo who ruled the realms of inspiration and imagination. Composers have long called upon the muses for help and insight. Music is not merely the result of emotions and pleasurable sensations, however.

Music is a discipline subject to formal study and analysis. It involves the juxtaposition of creative elements such as rhythm, melody, and harmony with intellectual aspects of composition, theory, and instrumentation. Like painters mixing red, blue, and yellow into thousands of colors, musicians blend these various elements to create classical symphonies, jazz improvisations, country ballads, and rock-and-roll tunes.

Throughout centuries of musical history, individual musical elements have been blended and modified in infinite ways. The resulting sounds may convey a whole range of moods, emotions, reactions, and messages. Music, then, is both an expression and reflection of human experience and emotion.

The foundations of modern musical styles were laid down by the first ancient musicians who used wood, rocks, animal skins—and their own bodies—to re-create the sounds of the natural world in which they lived. With their hands, their feet, and their very breath they ignited the passions of listeners and moved them to their feet. The dancing, in turn, had a mesmerizing and hypnotic effect that allowed people to transcend their worldly concerns. Through music they could achieve a level of shared experience that could not be found in other forms of communication. For this reason, music has always been part of religious endeavors, from ancient Egyptian religious ceremonies to modern Christian masses. And it has inspired dance movements from kings and queens spinning the minuet to punk rockers slamming together in a mosh pit.

By examining musical genres ranging from Western classical music to rock and roll, readers will find a new understanding of old music and develop an appreciation for new sounds. Books in Lucent's Music Library focus on the music, the musicians, the instruments, and on music's place in cultural history. The songs and artists examined may be easily found in the CD and sheet music collections of local libraries so that readers may study and enjoy the music covered in the books. Informative sidebars, annotated bibliographies, and complete indexes highlight the text in each volume and provide young readers with many opportunities for further discussion and research.

A Global Beat

The sounds of Latin America have had an enduring influence on many styles of music over the years. From the late nineteenth century to the modern age, the rhythmic beats of samba, rumba, mambo, tango, and salsa have played an important role in "Latinizing" popular music heard around the world. Given the size and diversity of Latin America, it is not surprising that its music has been so influential. The huge landmass that makes up Latin America contains nearly thirty countries and stretches from the southern border of the United States through parts of the Caribbean and down to the tip of Chile, not far from Antarctica. Within this area, nearly 800 million people speak several European languages and countless native dialects. Their music has drawn on a profusion of sounds, including African rhythms, Spanish song forms, European classical styles, American rock, and indigenous rhythms and harmonies.

These disparate elements, blended together over the course of centuries, have evolved into hundreds of musical styles. Yet each nation has its own distinctive and unique musical forms. For example, Cuban music is said to contain equal portions of African and Spanish influence with little from Amerindians. Peruvian music, by contrast, has strong Amerindian roots blended with Spanish styles and only a dash of African rhythm. Some Mexican music draws inspiration from traditional Spanish ballads that are put to the German polka beat.

The Latin Tinge in Popular Music

Many of these Latin genres have had a major impact on popular music, and their strongest influences were felt in jazz music, which originated in New Orleans in the early twentieth century. The city, once ruled by the Spanish, had long been a center of trade for people from Mexico, Cuba, Puerto

Rico, Venezuela, and Colombia. New Orleans was also home to black people whose ancestry stretched back to Africa, the Caribbean, and South America. In the 1910s, African American musicians such as Jelly Roll Morton adapted the rhythmic figures from Afro-Cuban upright bass and drum patterns to invent a new style of jazz called stride piano. This sound, which Morton called the "Latin Tinge,"[1] formed the foundation of New Orleans jazz, a musical style that took the world by storm in the 1920s and has inspired countless musicians since that time.

The Latin Tinge moved north to New York City in the 1930s when Argentinean immigrants introduced tango music and dancing to the American public. Tango musicians packed dance halls and sold millions of records after America's biggest movie star, Rudolph Valentino, performed the dance on the silver screen in 1920s films. The mambo and samba became similar fads in the 1940s and 1950s. Even the hits of rock and roll, the most commercially successful music form in history, were heavily influenced by the Latin Tinge, as Latino journalist and author Ed Morales writes in *The Latin Beat:*

[Funky] Latin rhythms thoroughly permeated American pop—Afro-Cuban piano figures form the basis of the Isley Brothers' *Twist and Shout*, and the five-beat rhythm that pervades Buddy

Holly's *Not Fade Away* . . . is essentially Afro-Cuban. . . . The Latin sound influenced the shaking and rattling behind rock and roll through New Orleans pianist/vocalist Fats Domino and the traces of *habanera* [Cuban dance music] found in the early stages of rockabilly. There were also musical influences from Mexico. The *corrido* tradition, based on Spanish ballads and important along the Texas-Mexico border, probably had an influence on . . . [Oklahoma folksinger] Woody Guthrie, Bob Dylan's forebear. The curious sound of the Farfisa organ, used as a novelty in late-1950s *conjunto* (Mexican-American popular dance group) music, would become a signature of American psychedelic music half a decade later.[2]

While the Latin Tinge influenced countless musicians, Latin performers have incorporated sounds of the north into their styles. In the past four decades, Latin players drew their inspiration not only from their traditional national sounds but also from the Beatles, Bob Dylan, the blues of the Mississippi Delta, and the cool jazz from California. In the twenty-first century, newer sounds continue to spice up the Latin Tinge, including European electronica dance music, Jamaican reggae, African soukous, and American hip-hop.

Throughout history, music has constantly evolved and changed in this way even as it has preserved elements of the past. Today, the story of Latin American music continues to progress. With their strong roots in Amerindian, African, European, and American cultures, the sounds emanating from Latin America will undoubtedly remain vital and significant for some time to come.

Chapter One

Roots Music

Many sounds heard in Latin American music today can be traced back centuries to Africa, Europe, and the Americas. African elements include traditional rhythm patterns and song structures that have been in use for thousands of years. The African sounds were later inspired by Europeans, who contributed a wide range of instruments along with specific poetic verse forms. Music in Spain was also strongly influenced by traveling musicians from as far away as India, North Africa, and the Middle East. From the Americas, indigenous peoples from Mexico to the Amazon rain forest have added their own ancient forms that include vocal harmony styles and musical scales. Taken together, these elements form the basis for Latin music heard today throughout the world.

The Aztec Influence

The oldest musical traditions in Latin America are based on the sounds of the Maya, Aztec, and Inca societies that once dominated Central and South America. Archaeologists have unearthed ancient musical instruments made from bone, wood, ceramics, and other materials. These items have allowed scholars called ethnomusicologists to speculate about the ancient music of the Americas in its cultural context. Their work is aided by the indigenous peoples throughout the region, who continue to play music using instruments similar to those played in ancient times.

The Amerindians of Central and South America played three types of music: music for pleasure that inspired group singing and dance; functional music such as work songs and martial music; and the largest category, religious music used for rituals, magic, and communication with supernatural forces.

One of the major indigenous musical influences in Central America may be traced to the Aztec people who, according to art historian Laurence E. Schmeckebier in *Modern Mexican Art*, lived in "well-planned cities with towering pyramids and impressive temples [and] . . . brilliantly colored palaces with extensive apartments and terraces." The Aztec culture also supported an "elaborate patronage of the arts such as poetry, the ritual dance, and music."[3]

The Aztec constructed a monetary system based on gold and copper coins that were highly coveted by Spanish conquistadores, led by Hernán Cortés, who arrived in present-day Mexico in March 1519. Within months,

In Aztec society, the use of varied, sophisticated musical instruments was central to worship and rituals.

the conquistadores were at war with the Aztec. In one early battle, the Aztec captured several enemy fighters and sacrificed them on an altar set atop a tall pyramid. In 1568, Spanish soldier Bernal Díaz, a soldier in Cortés's army, wrote *True History of the Conquest of New Spain*, in which he described the music the Aztec played during this bloody ceremony:

As we were retreating we heard the sound of trumpets from the great [altar] . . . which from its height dominates the whole City, and also a drum, a most dismal sound indeed it was, like an instrument of demons, as it resounded so that one could hear it two leagues [6 miles or 9.6 kilometers] off, and with it many small tambourines and shell trumpets, horns, and whistles. At that moment as we afterward learnt, they were offering the hearts of ten of our comrades. . . . Again there was sounded the dismal drum of Huichilobos [the Aztec god of sacrifice] and many other shells and horns and things like trumpets and the sound of them all was terrifying, and we all looked towards the lofty [altar] where they were being sounded, and saw our comrades whom they had captured . . . were being carried by force up the steps, and they were taking them to be sacrificed. . . . [After] they had danced they immediately placed them on their backs . . . and with stone knives they sawed open their chests and drew out their palpitating hearts and offered them to the idols. . . . The Mexicans offered great sacrifice and celebrated festivals every night at their great [altar] at Tlatelolco and sounded their cursed drum, trumpets, kettle drums and shells, and uttered yells and howls.[4]

Because the songs like those described by Díaz were designed to terrorize enemies such as the conquistadores, for the next four centuries the music of indigenous Mexicans was dismissed by authors and music scholars as barbaric and frightful. The musicologists based their judgment not on written musical scores, which did not exist, but on the sounds that could be produced from the instruments commonly used by the Aztec. In 1917, Alba Herrera y Ogazon, a member of the Mexican National Conservatory of Music, stated in *The Musical Art of Mexico* that these instruments are not "capable of producing either alone, or in conjunction with each other, a grateful harmony. . . . What these depraved sounds do conjure up are instead scenes of unrelieved ferocity."[5]

As Herrera and other researchers have learned, the Aztec made a wide variety of wind instruments. Flutes were crafted from clay, reeds, and even from human and animal bones. The conch shell was a particularly important instrument in war and used to

The Pyramid of the Sun was the focal point of Aztec religious ritual and ceremony in the ancient city of Teotihuacan.

issue warning blasts. Several conch shells blown simultaneously by trumpeters could be heard up to 10 miles (16km) away in mountainous terrain.

Ceremonial instruments such as rattles were made from gourds or drilled bones filled with pebbles. The rhythm instrument known as a rasp consisted of grooved surfaces cut into bone, over which a musician dragged a stick. There were also several types of drums, including the huehuetl, a horizontal drum on a three-legged stand played with fingers, and the teponaztli, a drum played with drumsticks.

In the years following the Spanish conquest, the surviving Amerindians in the region set aside these native instruments and skillfully adopted the violins, trumpets, and organs brought to Mexico by the conquerors. When not playing the songs Christian missionaries taught them, the Amerindians used the European instruments to play their traditional songs in secret. In this manner, indigenous and Spanish music began

Adapting Spanish Instruments

In 1615, Franciscan friar Juan de Torquemada described how the Aztec people adopted Spanish music and began constructing European instruments. The following excerpt from his book, Monarquia Indiana, *is quoted in Robert Stevenson's* Music in Aztec and Inca Territory*:*

The first instruments of music manufactured here were flutes, then oboes, and afterwards viols and bassoons and cornetts. After a while there was no single instrument used in churches which Indians in the larger towns had not learned to make and play. It became unnecessary to import any of these from Spain. One thing can be asserted without fear of contradiction; in all Christendom there is nowhere a greater abundance of flutes, sackbuts [early trombones], trumpets, and drums, than here which are administered by the orders. However, with these, not the Indians but rather Spanish builders have taken charge of construction, since the Indians do not have capital for such larger enterprises. The Indians make the organs under supervision, and they play the organs in our monasteries and convents. The other instruments which serve for solace or delight on secular occasions are all made here by the Indians, who also play them: rebecs [three-string bowed instruments], guitars, trebles, viols, harps, spinets.

Robert Stevenson, *Music in Aztec and Inca Territory.* Berkeley and Los Angeles: University of California Press, 1968, p. 172.

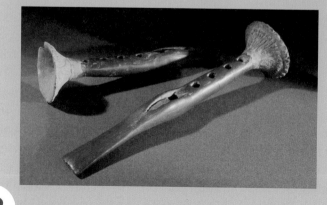

These flutes are typical examples of European instruments modified by the Aztecs.

to blend. This was the case not only with the Aztec but also with the indigenous Maya, who lived in southern Mexico, Guatemala, Honduras, and elsewhere.

In the twenty-first century, the Maya continue to play the old songs, having adapted them to European instruments such as the trumpet and guitar. A good example of this refashioned music may be heard on the Folkways album *Modern Mayan: The Indian Music of Chiapas, Mexico*, described by music scholar Richard Anderson: "The music of the indigenous people of the southern Mexican state of Chiapas reflects many varied influences, past and present. . . . [All] share their basic Mayan roots with both Aztec and Spanish borrowings."[6]

Incan and Peruvian Music

Like the Aztec in Mexico, the Inca who ruled present-day Bolivia, Ecuador, and Peru built a highly developed civilization with a strong musical legacy. Archaeologists have discovered a wide variety of flutes, drums, bone rasps, conch shells, and rattles throughout the region. According to Latin American and Caribbean music scholar Robert Stevenson in *The Music of Peru*, the "Andean peoples ruled by the Incas [perfected] the most advanced musical instruments known in either North or South America before Columbus's discovery."[7]

Flutes made from pelican, llama, puma, and deer bones were played alongside ocarinas, small, clay wind instruments with three finger holes.

The Inca also created trumpets from clay tubes as well as the skulls of dogs and deer. Like many other instruments created by Amerindians, the trumpets were both musical instruments and works of art decorated with religious symbols. In *The Music of Peru*, Stevenson describes a coiled clay trumpet, crafted to honor a cat god: "[A] feline juts out at one side of the [trumpet] bell. . . . Six stylized human heads rim the bell, their faces so turned that the three in each semicircle look towards the feline deity. Meanwhile his bulbous eyes peer above a mouthful of exposed teeth."[8]

In addition to flutes and trumpets, the Inca also used drums, which played an extremely important role in ceremonies, war, and long-distance communication. The largest drums were built from timber frames 9 to 11 feet (2.7 to 3.3m) across. The drumheads were made of leather and tied onto the wood with V-shaped thongs. Drummers could play distinct beats to convey messages to people as far as 9 miles (14km) away. The Inca used these mammoth drums in celebrations performed only for the most elite members of royalty. The drum was mounted on the backs of several people and beaten by a woman as three hundred dancers linked arms. In a special ritual, the dancers took three steps forward and two steps back as they slowly approached the king. Although the huge drums are not used today, weddings, dances, and other festivities are celebrated with fifty-member bands who beat large, deep-toned drums called bombos.

Perhaps the most well-known Inca instrument to survive to modern times is the panpipe, or antaras. This instrument features three to fifteen pipes of various lengths aligned in a row, each tube capable of producing a single note. Antaras were originally made from clay, but modern instruments may be bamboo or wood. The pipes can be made of different lengths or

A Peruvian flute player makes music on an instrument that remains virtually unchanged since the time of the Inca.

tunings to allow musicians to play scales of five, six, or seven notes.

Using antaras, drums, and flutes, the Quechua people of Peru, Ecuador, and Bolivia continue to play their traditional songs. Living in isolated regions, the Amerindian musicians produce music that is diverse and unique to each small village and relies on different scales, song structures, and playing styles. The sounds might also be flavored with varying musical styles of European origin.

Most people outside of Peru have not heard the music as it is played by the Amerindians. However, Peruvian folk bands have become ubiquitous in tourist towns and on college campuses in Europe, Canada, Japan, and North America. These musicians, dressed in ponchos and other traditional garb, play panpipes, bombos, guitars, charangos (a ten-string guitar), and notched-end flutes called quenas. One piece most of these poncho bands play is an arrangement of the eighteenth-century Peruvian folk anthem "El Cóndor Pasa." The song was popularized in 1970 by the American pop duo Simon and Garfunkel who recorded the song with Quechua musicians for the best-selling album *Bridge over Troubled Water*.

Music of the Orinoco Delta

The native music of Peru heard today has been changing and evolving since the Spanish arrived. However, there are parts of Mesoamerica so isolated that European and African styles have had little influence on the sounds of the indigenous peoples. Nonetheless, recordings of songs played by the Amerindian dwellers of the rain forest have inspired nonindigenous musicians, who have either adapted the music to their modern sounds or incorporated it directly as digital samples on CDs. Whatever its influence, indigenous roots music remains an important part of Latin America's cultural heritage.

The Warao, who live deep within the Amazon rain forest in Venezuela and have had only sporadic contact with outsiders, are an example of a people whose ancient musical traditions have remained unchanged for millennia. These twenty thousand or so inhabitants, whose name translates as "canoe people," live in houses built on stilts over isolated swampy islands in the Orinoco River delta. As is true among many indigenous cultures, music is central to Warao life, and almost everybody sings as they work, play, and relax. Work songs, called dakotutuma, are sung for various tasks. Men sing special dakotutuma when they paddle canoes, which is often since it is the only form of transportation available to these river people.

Women have dakotutuma for gathering and cooking foods. Lullabies are particularly important, as these songs are meant to impart educational information to children. Director of the Center for Music of the Americas Dale A. Olsen explains in the article "An Introduction to the Music and

Culture of the Warao Indians of Venezuela":

Many of the Warao lullabies describe animals and spirits of the rain forest, most of them poten-tially dangerous. The majority of the animal lullabies are about jaguars: some refer to the physical characteristics of the jaguar, while others are about the jaguar's desire to eat babies. The song texts often

This Quechua man of Peru examines a panpipe, or antaras, that is used to play traditional ethnic music.

Inca Songs of
Love and Loss

In 1613, Peru native Huamán Poma de Ayala wrote a 1,179-page book about Inca culture as it was at the time of the Spanish conquest in 1533. Quoted in The Music of Peru *by Robert Stevenson, Poma de Ayala describes a type of indigenous love song called a haravi whose themes would doubtlessly be familiar to listeners of Latin music today:*

When the haravi is sung . . . [the] pangs of love form their most frequent theme. The singer in a typical haravi complains that unlucky chance separates him from his beloved who is as beautiful as the yellow mountain-flower of the Andes. . . . But though apart, he always thinks of her and pursues her like a precious but elusive reflection in the water. Her deceitful mother seeks to separate them. Her evil father also tries to keep them apart. But perhaps the Maker of All will one day take pity and reunite them. Even now when he thinks of her smiling eyes he loses his senses. He has been searching everywhere for her, traversing mountains, rivers, and villages. Now he can only sit and weep.

Quoted in Robert Stevenson, *The Music of Peru*. Washington, DC: Pan American Union, 1960, p. 141.

tell the infant to go to sleep or it will be eaten by a supernatural jaguar (or some other infant-eating animal or spirit).[9]

Such lullabies serve to warn babies about the dangers found in the rain forest or describe poisonous plants that children should avoid. Others explain the types of work performed by adults so that a child will expect to perform those tasks when he or she grows up. Research has shown that such lullabies also help infants learn to speak and understand their native language.

Supernatural Communication

The majority of Warao songs are categorized as theurgy, or supernatural communication. These songs often concern matters of birth, death, war, hunting, and healing. Joyous songs for fertility and harvesting are sung by all members of the tribe, while those written to address cosmic events are sung only by religious healers called shamans. The shamans specialize in curing spiritual and physical ailments through chanting, praying, and singing. The healing songs are used to communicate with good and evil spirits. These songs, said to be composed by the deities themselves, are passed down from one generation to the next or might be revealed to a shaman in a dream.

Shamans almost always accompany themselves with a special rattle, an instrument said to be a very powerful curing tool. These rattles have so much significance that shamans believe that they or their family members will die if the rattle is lost, stolen, or destroyed.

The Warao use other types of rattles as well for spiritual purposes. One type, called a sewei, consists of small hooves, seeds, nuts, or even giant beetle wings strung together. This instrument, attached to a pole or worn around the ankle or wrist, makes a shaking sound during dance rituals. According to Warao belief, a vision of the first sewei came to a shaman during a dream, and since that time only the most important people in the village are allowed to own one. Several other types of rattles are made from gourds mounted on sticks. These might be filled with nuts or seeds to make them rattle, although the most spiritually significant rattles are filled with small quartz crystals and decorated with parrot feathers, which are believed to hold magical powers.

A Warao woman of the Orinoco River delta paddles her canoe. The Warao of Venezuela have had little contact with outsiders.

Unlike many indigenous tribes, the Warao only have one type of drum, a double-headed ehuru drum in the shape of an hourglass, made from a hollow log. The drumhead is made from monkey or jaguar skin, and the drummer plays the instrument with a drumstick fashioned from a small tree branch.

Flutes made from deer bones and cane reeds are also common. The most sacred wind instrument among the Warao is the isimoi, an unusual instrument made from a long, tubelike reed threaded through an oblong gourd. The sound of the instrument is similar to the high-pitched whistles of birds in the forest. Similar single-reed instruments are made by other indigenous peoples in the region, including the Wai-Wai, the Yekuana, and Guajiro.

The Warao also have several types of stringed instruments. During times of relaxation, singers may accompany themselves on a handmade violin called a sekeseke or on a four-stringed guitarlike instrument called a wandora.

The Afro-Spanish Connection

The musical culture of indigenous South Americans is similar to that found in Africa, where people have been incorporating music into work, play, and spiritual purposes for thousands of years. Like the Warao,

Africans have songs for nearly every occasion. Not only do they sing educational lullabies to babies, but they have music for punishment as well. For example, the Akan of Ghana have special drums that are beaten as a petty thief is marched through the streets of a village. These musical traditions traveled to Latin America with black slaves who were first brought to Mesoamerica in the sixteenth century.

The Africans in Latin America came from at least two thousand tribes that spoke more than twenty-four hundred different languages. This diversity produced not only an incredible

Making a Bone Flute

The Warao people of Venezuela play flutes made from deer tibia when traveling, dancing, or gathering ceremonial herbs from the rain forest. Similar flutes are played by indigenous people throughout Latin America. In Music of the Warao of Venezuela, *Dale A. Olsen describes how the flutes, called muhusemoi, are made:*

After he has selected the proper deer tibia, the maker opens both ends of the bone and removes as much marrow as he can with his knife. Then he places the bone in a place out of the reach of dogs but within the reach of cockroaches, which eat out the marrow within several days. After the bone is hollowed and dried, the maker forms the saddle-shaped mouthpiece with a knife. Then he places the mouthpiece edge within the crotch between his thumb and first finger, using his fingers as rulers for finger-hole placement. Where the tip of his first finger falls he will drill the bottom finger hole with the sharpened point of a harpoon . . . a technique requiring only about one minute of effort per finger hole depending on the sharpness of the harpoon point. The maker then measures the distance for the second finger hole with the back of his thumb (from the tip of the thumb to the first joint) and drills it with similar ease. The same techniques are used to determine the placement of the third finger hole and drill it out. Because Warao hands and Orinoco Delta deer tibias all differ in size, there is naturally a difference in the tone system of the final product.

Dale A. Olsen, *Music of the Warao of Venezuela.* Gainesville: University Press of Florida, 1996, pp. 78–79.

Instruments such as this elaborately decorated Peruvian flute are historically made of animal bone such as deer tibia.

array of musical styles but also a wide variety of instruments, such as rattles, woodwinds, drums, and stringed instruments. Most significant, however, are vocal traditions, as music producer and African music expert John Storm Roberts writes in *Black Music of Two Worlds*:

> [The] human voice is . . . of overriding importance; call-and-response singing is by far the most common form of group vocal technique. African music is often built up by the use of relatively short musical phrases, often repeated, or of longer lines made up of phrases never repeated in just the same form. Rhythm and, more generally, a

percussive approach are fundamental. And above all, music is a communal functional expression to a far greater degree than in most other parts of the world.[10]

The storied African rhythmic and communal song traditions were transformed themselves as they were taken to other lands by wandering traders. Their connection to Latin America occurred through a series of historical events that began in the early eighth century on the Iberian Peninsula, the location of present-day Spain and Portugal.

Between 711 and 1492, the Moors from Morocco in North Africa ruled Iberia, which was a center of world commerce and culture during that

Far from their origins, the African instruments shown in this illustration were brought to Latin America through commercial trade.

time. The traveling merchants who conducted business were Roman Christians, Palestinian Jews, North African Arabs, African blacks, and eastern European Gypsies. When these people socialized, they traded musical instruments and styles from their native regions. Musicians from the Middle East brought flutes and early versions of violins as well as the laud, a stringed instrument that was later transformed into the lute and guitar. Africans brought their own stringed instruments and a wide variety of drums, rattles, and other rhythm instruments. In this milieu, traditional song styles were traded as eagerly as the food, tools, and cloth that were the basis of commerce at the time. In *The Latin Beat*, Ed Morales describes this musical blend and how it has endured in traditional Latin song forms:

Spain, like much of Europe, was overrun by various wandering tribes. The gypsy tradition, which originated in northern India, brought a sense of nomadic loss to Iberia, and the characteristic vocal trill (vibrato) from North African Arabic culture . . . seemed to belong to a similar emotional register. The troubadour influence from France, in the twelfth and thirteenth centuries, became central in Spanish literature and greatly affected its song forms. By the sixteenth century, the troubadours of [Spain] were also declaiming in the . . . decima style, featuring ten lines of eight syllables each, that was pioneered by a mixed culture of Spaniards and Arabs who often spoke a hybrid language known as Mozárabic during the Moorish occupation.[11]

The decima song pattern was adapted by African drummers because of the interestingly repetitive rhythm of the lyrics. The decima was also taken by Spanish sailors and traders to the Canary Islands off the coast of Africa, where it was adopted by the mixed-race population composed of indigenous African and Spanish cultures. Many people from the Canary Islands were part of the Spanish migration to the New World, and they took this song form with them. In the nineteenth and twentieth centuries, the decima influenced a wide variety of Latin styles. According to Morales: "The décima form survives today in the modern Latin ballad, known as bolero, the Mexican corrido, the Colombian vallenato, the Puerto Rican décima or seis, the Cuban trova, and even the folk songs of Argentine nueva cancion."[12]

From Africa to the Aztec and the Inca, the forebears of Latin music have circled the globe for hundreds of years. The unique melodies and instruments played important roles in ancient societies, and they continue to influence millions of musicians in the twenty-first century.

Chapter Two

Caribbean Spice

In 1492, when Christopher Columbus sailed from Spain to the Caribbean islands with sailors of European, African, and Middle Eastern descent, he unknowingly set in motion a mixing of world musical cultures that continues to this day. In the centuries that followed, a multiracial mix of people flooded into the Caribbean from Spain, France, England, the Canary Islands, and African nations such as Egypt, Ghana, Nigeria, Senegal, and Benin. Each group brought its own musical traditions, many of which were eventually mixed and blended into modern Latin musical styles.

Cuban Musical Culture

In the early sixteenth century, when the Spanish colonizers began to arrive in the New World in large numbers, the Taino occupied the island of Cuba. At that time, the primary percussion instruments of the Taino and the other original inhabitants of the Caribbean,

the Carib Indians, were maracas and guiros. Maracas are rattles traditionally made from small gourds mounted on sticks and filled with pebbles or seeds. A larger gourd with parallel notches cut into it, the guiro, or scraper, is played by a percussionist rubbing a wooden stick over the notches to produce a danceable, ratchetlike sound.

The Spanish annihilated the native population by 1550, but guiros and maracas found a place in the music played by the new arrivals. In the following years, Spanish settlers brought the guitar, the twelve-string laud, and the three-string bandurria to Cuba, along with a variety of woodwinds, brass horns, and drums. The Spanish also imported thousands of African slaves from the nations of Benin, Nigeria, Congo, and Cameroon. These people, many of Yoruba descent, brought their own musical traditions based on group drumming, singing, and dancing. By the time slavery was abolished in Cuba in 1886, more than 1 million people of African descent were living on the island.

The mix of European and African cultures in the booming New World colonies created a musical stew composed of many ingredients. The Creole settlers (Caribbean-born people of Spanish descent) particularly enjoyed military bands that featured trumpets, clarinets, fifes, and drums. These bands played at all official ceremonies and during celebrations on special occasions. Church music was another important style in Cuba, and motets and hymns were played on Sundays and religious holidays. Musicians playing organs, bassoons, flutes, oboes, viols, and violins backed church choirs.

Secular music also blossomed in Cuba, and by the early nineteenth century, there were at least fifty public dance halls in the capital of Havana. Since the musicians who played the halls were paid poorly or not at all, few Creoles played in Cuban dance

Spanish colonizers adopted rattles called maracas from original Caribbean inhabitants. Maracas are still used in modern Latin music.

bands. Instead, the work was performed by slaves and free blacks. Moreover, from the very early years of colonization, both church orchestras and military bands used black and mixed race, or mulatto, musicians. In 1800, musician Antonio Valle Hernández commented on this phenomenon: "The arts which, in other countries, are the occupation of respected, well-born white people, here are the near-monopoly of people of color."[13]

As often happens with poorly paid musicians, Cuba's performers learned to play all styles of music to improve their chances of finding gigs. Maya Roy, musicologist at the University of Paris, explains in *Cuban Music:*

> For most of the musicians of color, the boundaries between classical, religious, and popular music were blurred, since they were proficient in all three types. With their instrumental expertise and their [African] musical heritage, musicians of color created original scores with a typical Creole flavor that won over the popular public, and then fashionable high society as well.[14]

Music of the Gods

Even as black musicians were gaining acceptance for their Creolized music, many also maintained their Yoruban traditions. Although the Spanish baptized all slaves into Roman Catholicism, they also allowed them to practice their traditional religions, which were centered on drumming and dancing. As they had done with music, Cuba's black population blended traditional African and Spanish religious practices. This melding of spiritual beliefs produced a religion called Santeria, whose practitioners worshipped deities, or orishas, that combined characteristics of Yoruban gods with those of Catholic saints.

Dispensing with church organs and choirs, Santeria worship was centered around a two-headed drum called the bata. Then as now, these drums are always played in threes, in sets consisting of a large, medium, and small drum. The rim of the largest, lowest-pitched drum, the iya, is fitted with small brass bells that enhance the drum's sound. The medium bata is called the itotele, and the smallest, highest-pitched drum is called the okonkolo. Since each drum can produce two tones from its double heads, a set of bata can emit six tones. Each of these tones may be modified by the intensity of the slap and the location where the drumhead is hit.

This complex array of drum tones is important to Santeria worship because practitioners believe each orisha can be called down to earth only with a unique musical pattern called a toque. Ceremonies open with the lead drummer playing a toque on the iya for a specific orisha. The itotele player plays a counterpoint to the iya, and the okonkolo begins a steady rhythm pattern. Roy describes the importance of this ritual:

Preserving African Traditions

In Cuba, the Spanish instituted a system of dividing slaves by their region, town, or tribal origins. Called *cabildos*, these fraternities were mutual aid societies that taught newcomers from Africa how to live within Cuba's slave system. Although the Spanish founded the *cabildos* to defuse tensions between slaves and their owners, the organizations served as cultural institutions that enabled slaves to preserve their traditional music, songs, dances, and religious beliefs.

Each *cabildo* was organized into a social hierarchy under which members elected a king or queen to lead the group. The *cabildos*, with names like the Cabildo of the Royal Congos, met in temples where magical objects devoted to the gods, or orishas, were displayed. Members of the *cabildos* played drums and danced while wearing costumes and masks. On Spanish religious holidays, such as Epiphany or Corpus Christi, the slaves were allowed to perform in the streets. Although the *cabildos* were meant to divide the slaves into separate ethnic groups, people intermingled in urban areas. Through this blending of cultures, new and unique music emerged.

Sacred and consecrated instruments . . . these drums speak; they are the voice that calls the deities, and the divinities speak through the drums. Initially, the combination of rhythmic patterns, melodic inflections, and timbres reproduced the tonal sequences of the Yoruba language. There is a special musical language of the drums that corresponds to each divinity, as well as special songs and dances. . . . The *olubatá* [drummers] who play the sacred drums—the only ones authorized to ritually consecrate them—have passed down, over the centuries, an extremely complex body of knowledge: a multitude of melodic/rhythmic patterns, as well as the skill of making the transition from one rhythmic pattern to another in a conversation with the same divinity or in going from one invocation to another.[15]

Men create rhythm on different percussion instruments during a Santeria celebration. Each orisha, or deity, is summoned to Earth by its own particular toque, or musical pattern.

By the middle of the twentieth century, the musical and religious traditions of Santeria had spread beyond Cuba to Puerto Rico and into the United States, especially New York City and Miami. Santeria chants, sung in the Yoruba language, have been recorded by Latin music stars including Celia Cruz and Mongo Santamaria, and even white rockers such as David Byrne from the group Talking Heads.

Let's Get Going

In Cuba, the Santeria rhythms were also played in a secularized form called rumba. Unlike the ritual music of Santeria, in which specific beats are played on low-pitched drums, the rumba beat is improvised on high-pitched percussion instruments.

Rumba was originally played on streets and at parties by tradespeople working in Havana. The name of this exciting and passionate music literally means "form a path," or in street slang, "let's get going." Rumba originated among Cuba's poorest citizens—workers who used whatever tools were at hand to play rumba rhythms. Farm workers set a beat with hoes and shovels; dock workers whacked packing crates, or *cajóns*, with tools. Bakers beat out the rumba rhythms on flour crates with their fists and cooking utensils. The rumba performance is described by author and documentary filmmaker Isabelle Leymarie in *Cuban Fire* as "a complex and gripping ritual including drumming, singing, declamation and dancing [that] thrives in back alleys and courtyards, where African blood

Packing-Crate Percussion

Rumba rhythms originated in the working-class black communities in Havana in the 1890s. As Maya Roy writes in Cuban Music, *rumba players were able to fashion remarkable percussion instruments from the packing crates they found in their workplaces:*

The first . . . percussion instruments were large wooden crates of varying shapes, known by the generic name of *cajón*. The musicians generally preferred the crates used for shipping codfish and, for the smallest instruments, the crates for packing candles. The wooden parts would be cut out and polished to improve their resonance; then they were rejoined with nails or glue. Later, cajóns were made for a specifically musical usage, in different sizes, whose forms might vary but generally go in sets of three according to the established arrangement of their rhythmic and sound relationship. In fact, this arrangement is the only criterion that permits a classification of these instruments, especially since the names given to them by musicians, according to their use, often vary.

The stable rhythmic pattern is established by the *tumbador* (or *salidor*), the largest of the *cajóns*, which the musician plays seated. The instrument is beaten according to different styles (including with a closed fist) on the sides or on one side and on the front, with one hand playing in counterpoint to the other. The small *cajón*, also called *repicador*, is used for improvising. The musician holds it in place by squeezing it between the knees. The last *cajón*, of a middle register, is called *tres-dos;* it is linked rhythmically to the *tumbador*.

Maya Roy, *Cuban Music*. Princeton, NJ: Markus Wiener, 2002, p. 51.

courses strongly in the veins of the inhabitants."[16]

During the twentieth century, drums and rattles of all shapes and sizes, especially upright congas, replaced packing crates. Hardwood blocks known as claves also became central to rumba rhythm. These long dowels were originally used as pegs to join boards in shipbuilding. Claves are struck in patterns of either two beats followed by three beats or the reverse, three beats followed by two. This sets a steady and unchanging rhythm pattern that keeps the drummers on beat while giving the music an expressive charge. Cuban musical historian Fernando Ortiz explains the significance of the clave:

> Aside from its rhythmic importance in musical practice, the Cuban clave is itself, by virtue of its simplicity and striking timbre, a melodic exclamation filled with emotion. . . . There is something about [the clave] that eludes the typical opaque sound of wood. . . . Its vibrations create an almost crystalline or metallic resonance.[17]

Cuban rumba players set the beat with intricate polyrhythms, in which several different rhythms and beats weave around and intertwine with one another. A lead singer, called *El Gallo*, or the Rooster, crows improvised lyrics above the cacophonous cadence of the percussion. Lyrics are patterned in stanzas of four lines called quatrains or in eight-syllable, ten-line verses based on Spanish decima song patterns. At first, the lyrics often incorporated news from the streets, political satire, and commentary about current events. Group participation was originally key to the rumba and used the traditional African call-and-response technique, in which the singer sang out a line and the other musicians and audience members repeated the line together in a chorus.

Music as insistently rhythmic as rumba inspired a dance, also called the rumba. There are three styles of rumba dance. The yambu can be slow and hypnotic, while the guaguanco is a fast dance featuring couples who perform provocative moves such as pelvic thrusting. The columbia, also a fast dance, is performed only by men, who often aggressively joust and parry in mock knife fights.

The Rise of Son

As rumba was developing in Cuba's urban areas, another form of percussion-only music, called son, evolved in the mountainous Oriente Province in eastern Cuba. The first son musicians were rural workers who combined syncopated African rhythms with melody lines that were independent of the percussive beat. Son has several similarities to rumba: The music follows a constant beat set down by a clave player, and it has a ten-line decima lyric pattern.

In the late 1800s, Nené Manfugas brought the sounds of son montuno, or son of the mountains, to Santiago in

A woman dances the rumba in a Havana city street. The rumba beat is derived from sacred Santeria toque rhythms.

east Cuba. Manfugas played a guitar-like instrument called a tres, which has three double strings. Son bands also added bongos, maracas, singers, and guitars to perform the fast-paced rhythmic music. By the 1910s, son sound had spread to Havana, carried by migrating agricultural workers and day laborers. As music that originated among the poor, son was at first condemned as decadent by the government and upper-class citizens of the capital. However, son continued to flourish, and by the end of the 1920s, many son orchestras had grown to in-clude six or seven players, including trumpeters and bassists. The joyful sounds emanating from these sextets and septets proved to be irresistible to Havana's most affluent citizens, and son soon emerged as the national sound of the Cuban people.

The red-hot dance group Sexteto Habenero, featuring a pair of lead vocalists and a sizzling trumpet, was the first to achieve widespread popularity in Havana. The group's records were sold in the United States and Europe, and son quickly achieved international popularity. Hollywood soon picked up on the trend. In the 1930s, the movie *Cuban Love Song* featured the orchestra led by famed Cuban pianist and composer Ernesto Lecuona, while the film *Rumba*, with bandleader Xavier Cugat, introduced Cuban son music to countless Americans.

The son fad ended abruptly in 1959 when Communist dictator Fidel Castro took control of Cuba, prompting the U.S. government to institute an embargo against the nation. As their record sales and international gigs dried up, Cuba's most talented son musicians were suddenly unemployed. Many eventually died or disappeared. In 1995, however, a few remaining son musicians, many of them past eighty years of age, were contacted by slide guitar player and Los Angeles native Ry Cooder, who had traveled to Cuba to learn about the musical style.

When Cooder played with the old musicians, he was amazed to find that they had retained their musical skills despite long years of working menial jobs. Cooder contacted arranger Juan de Marcos Gonzalez to make a record with the veterans. In 1996, the album *Buena Vista Social Club*, featuring master vocalists Ibrahim Ferrer, Omara Portuondo, and Pio Leyva; Afro-Cuban pianist Rubén González; bassist Orlando "Cachaito" López; tres player Eliades Ochoa; and trumpeter Manuel "Guajiro" Mirabal, was released to widespread acclaim. The album eventually sold more than 2 million copies, and demand for the group was so great that a tour of Europe and the United States followed, ending at the famed Carnegie Hall in New York City. *Buena Vista Social Club* won several Grammys, and in 1999, director Wim Wenders released a film of the same name, which documents the recording of the album and parts of the concert tour. The popular record and film set off a Cuban music explosion in the late 1990s, and the son style once again was embraced by listeners around the globe.

The Afro-Cuban Spice Hits New York

The music featured in *Buena Vista Social Club* recalled a time when other forms of Cuban music in addition to

Bandleader Xavier Cugat played a huge part in popularizing Latin music in the United States, helping it achieve mainstream acceptance.

The Cuban ensemble Buena Vista Social Club performs onstage in Turkey in 2000. Thanks to a 1996 album featuring these musicians, Cuban son music exploded in popularity.

son were wildly popular in the United States. These styles caught the public's attention after World War II, when New York City was a prime destination for Cuban performers who combined Latin rhythms and melodies with big band jazz and swing. The resulting style, called Afro-Cuban jazz, was popularized by Cuban musicians such as Mario Bauza and Frank Raul Grillo, known as Machito. Their sound attracted African American jazz musicians, including trumpeter Dizzy Gillespie, who helped popularize the music among a wider audience. As Gillespie stated:

> I really became interested in bringing Latin and especially Afro-Cuban influences into my music. . . . No one was playing that type of music. . . . No one was doing that. I became very

fascinated with the possibilities for expanding and enriching jazz rhythmically and phonically through the use of Afro-Cuban rhythmic and melodic devices.[18]

As Gillespie was incorporating the Latin sounds into American jazz, a new dance rhythm called the cha-cha-cha in Havana made its way to New York. This new conga-driven sound soon acquired the name mambo, and New York dancers quickly fell into the fevered grip of "mambo mania."

The epicenter of this fad, the Palladium Ballroom in midtown Manhattan, was often packed with movie stars, jazz musicians, sports figures, and a multicultural mix of African Americans, Hispanics, and European Americans. Dancers competed to attract the most attention with ferocious acrobatics, moving to the sounds of Machito's

Afro-Cuban Orchestra, the Mambo Aces; Tito Rodriguez; and others. Tito Puente, known as the King of Mambo, or *El Rey*, was one of the most popular acts. Puente was a percussionist, arranger, and bandleader who eventually recorded a hundred albums, published more than four hundred compositions, and won four Grammy Awards. He was credited with introducing the timbales, double tom-tom drums played with sticks, to the Afro-Cuban sound. He also played trap drums, conga drums, claves, piano, and occasionally, saxophone and clarinet.

Spice It Up a Little

When the Palladium closed in the mid-1960s, the Afro-Cuban fad had run its course. By this time, however, millions of immigrants from Puerto Rico were living in New York, and a new sound was developing in the Puerto Rican neighborhood known as the Barrio. This sound, called salsa, incorporated Cuban son, Puerto Rican plena, Dominican merengue, mambo, rumba, and American rock and roll, soul, and funk.

The term *salsa*, or "sauce," was first used in a musical context by renowned Cuban composer and singer Ignacio Piñeiro, who wrote the hit son song "Enchale Salsita" in 1937. The song's title means "spice it up a little." Piñeiro wrote the song referring not to music but to the bland American food that he was served while on tour in the United States. Nonetheless, soon after the song was released, dancers in New York nightclubs began using the term to urge bands to add some hot Latin spice to their music. By the mid-1970s, there was plenty of spice in the salsa music of New York. Bands were playing the driving, danceable musical style in groups featuring claves, piano, bass, guitars, trumpets, conga, timbales, bongos, and even cowbells.

With its broad mix of musical forms, salsa is difficult to describe. However, as New York sociologist Vernon W. Boggs writes in *Salsiology*, the music is defined by the poverty and hopelessness many Puerto Rican immigrants face in the United States:

Salsa . . . represents a new phase in the evolution of Afro-Hispanic culture: that of the urban-industrial working class. The backbone of salsa music is the Puerto Rican [industrial wage earner]—and its counterparts in other major Caribbean cities. . . . The best salsa songs voice the problems of this disadvantaged class. Scarcity, violence, inequality, marginality, and desperation are translated into the words and music of the popular singers and performers from the barrio. Street fights and love affairs marked by treason and suspicion have replaced the romantic themes of [traditional Puerto Rican music]. The world of salsa is full of allusions to the factory, the supermarket, welfare programs, or urban decay. . . . Musically, salsa is as far removed

Mambo king Tito Puente is shown here playing percussion in the early days of his long, influential career melding American music with Afro-Cuban sounds.

from the cha-cha-cha as is the trombone from the violin: the carefully arranged sound of the latter has yielded to the violent orchestration of the former. The pace of life has quickened, and so has the rhythm of the music.[19]

The tough life of the Latino Barrio was a strong influence on one of the

Salsa pioneer Willie Colón checks a sound board in this undated photo. The renowned trombonist learned the feel of Puerto Rican music from his grandmother.

founding fathers of the salsa movement, trombonist Willie Colón. Born in the heart of the Latino Bronx in 1950, as a child Colón learned the lyrics to traditional Puerto Rican folk songs from his grandmother as she rocked him to sleep every night. After Colón signed with New York's Fania record label at the age of seventeen, his first album sold three hundred thousand copies. With this unprecedented success behind him, Colón continued to innovate. In the late 1960s, he was the first to use the trombone as a lead instrument. Colón also wrote music that placed less emphasis on the traditional clave beat while incorporating dance rhythms from Colombia, Panama, Brazil, Cuba, and Puerto Rico.

Since that time, Colón has collaborated with musical giants such as the Fania All Stars, Héctor LaVoe, and Celia Cruz, the singer known as the Queen of Salsa. In 1978, Colón collaborated with Panamanian poet, singer, and movie star Rubén Blades. Their album of socially conscious songs, *Siembra*, is the best-selling salsa album in history.

Salsa Romantica

During the 1980s, salsa lyrics with overt political content fell out of style and were replaced by a new form called salsa romantica, or romantic salsa. This music featured handsome singers with soft, smooth delivery who crooned sentimental lyrics about love at a slow, sensuous tempo. In 1986, singer Lalo Rodriguez defined the style with the international hit "Ven, Devórame Otra Vez" ("Come and Devour Me Again"). According to Morales, the song "establishes the basic narrative strategy of the salsa romantica [singer]: I am incapable of resisting a beautiful woman, and I hope that she will give herself to me, because otherwise I might die right here and now."[20] The sentiments expressed by Rodriguez proved to be irresistible to the record-buying public, and several salsa romantica singers have sold millions of records internationally.

Changes in salsa music were paralleled by changes in record production, which, by the end of the 1980s, was made cheaper and easier by the introduction of digital recording equipment. During this era, the center of Latin music production shifted from New York to Miami and San Juan, Puerto Rico. The Miami salsa influence was nowhere more obvious than in the music of Gloria Estefan's Miami Sound Machine. Estefan, born in Cuba, grew up in Miami in the 1960s and formed the Miami Sound Machine with her husband, Emilio, in 1979. By the mid-1980s, the group was one of the top bands in the United States, playing a mix of Latin salsa rhythms, disco, soul, and rock.

Estefan, who began a solo career in 1990, was hugely responsible for introducing Latin music styles to pop audiences. Her success spawned a new wave of extremely successful Latin crossover artists. One of them, Marc Anthony, born Marco Antonio Muniz in New York's Barrio, grew up listening to American soul music as well as Rubén Blades and Willie Colón. Anthony's big break came when he was hired as a backup singer for the teen pop sensation Backstreet Boys. In 1991, Anthony decided to return to his salsa roots, left the Backstreet Boys, and began recording salsa in Spanish. By 2000, after recording four albums in Spanish and two in English, Anthony was one of the top international stars of Latin music.

Merengue

As salsa music experienced an explosive popularity in the 1980s, the lively beat of merengue attracted devotees in the smaller clubs of New York City. Merengue evolved in the Dominican Republic among the rural people of Congo African heritage. The music was originally played on an accordion, a bass, the tambora drum, and the guira, a rattle made from the metal of a 5-gallon (19-liter) gas can. Other merengue instruments included guitars and a bass instrument called a marimbula, similar to the thumb piano with seven metal keys. Merengue musicians play an infectious, fast-paced, dance music featuring a 2/4 time signature with a strong emphasis on the first beat of every two bars.

Merengue became the national music and dance style of the Dominican Republic after it was promoted by president Rafael Trujillo in the 1930s. In the 1970s, the sound was transported to New York by Dominican immigrants who settled in Washington Heights. When the salsa craze hit New York, merengue bands often shared the concert-hall stage with salsa bands. In the 1980s, the merengue sound was modernized by Wilfrido "El Barbarazo" Vargas, who added rock, soul, jazz, reggae, and Brazilian samba songs to the musical mix. This style of playing other songs with merengue rhythms is known as fusilamento, or "shooting." In the twenty-first century, merengue has been fused with hip-hop, techno music, electronic sampling, and other modern techniques to create a new, ultra-fast fusilamento style.

Anthony, Estefan, and other singers helped make salsa mainstream music even as lesser known stars began experimenting with the sound. During the past several decades, salsa has blended with Latin rap and hip-hop. Groups such as Dark Latin Groove have pumped up the bass and sped up the rhythms to create a totally new sound called salsa gorda, or fat salsa. Meanwhile, new musical ingredients are being added to salsa every day in the United States, Cuba, Colombia, Puerto Rico, and Venezuela. Like other Caribbean sounds with roots in the nineteenth century, salsa has become an international music with a reach far beyond its humble roots.

Chapter Three

Brazilian Beats

There are few countries in which music is as important to the national soul as Brazil. Because Brazil has the largest black population of any nation outside of Africa, its music is heavily influenced by complex African musical traditions from the Yoruba, Fon, Ewe, Bantu, Ashanti, and Hausa peoples. Since the late nineteenth century, these ancient musical roots have merged with indigenous and Portuguese elements to form the modern Brazilian sounds of samba, bossa nova, and other styles. This music has enjoyed an international exposure that has placed Brazil among the top record-producing nations in the world.

Brazil differs from the rest of Latin America because it was settled largely by the Portuguese rather than the Spanish. Consequently, Brazil's non-indigenous people speak Portuguese. The nation also celebrates Carnaval, one of the most elaborate and untamed spring festivals in the world. During the five-day celebration, the country shuts down as thousands of costumed celebrants take to the streets to dance, drink, and parade in the days before Lent. Samba is the soundtrack to Carnaval, and this infectious rhythmic sound can be traced back five centuries to a time when Brazil was a nation of black slaves and Portuguese slave masters.

African Roots

The first African slaves were imported to Brazil in 1538. When the slave trade ended in 1850, more than 3.5 million Africans had survived the brutal journey across the Atlantic to Brazil—six times more than were taken to the United States. Before slavery was abolished in Brazil in 1888, the country's population included descendents of enslaved peoples from Sudan, Nigeria, Angola, the Congo, and Ghana. These people inherited music, dances, instruments, languages, and traditions from the

African continent. This unique Afro-Brazilian culture became intertwined with Amerindian heritage and Portuguese society through intermarriage. By the nineteenth century, most Brazilians were of a multicultural background that blended musical traditions from three continents.

One of those traditions, samba, has its roots in an ancient drumming and circular dance ritual called the bataque, originally performed by Brazilian slaves. The bataque featured call-and-response vocals, individuals dancing within a circle of singers, and an enthusiastic rhythmic clapping by spectators and participants. Although the bataque was originally a religious dance, slaves disguised it as a secular celebration because the Portuguese forbade the Africans to practice their sacred beliefs.

Anti-African prohibitions also forced black Brazilians to disguise their traditional religious practices by merging them with Roman Catholicism. For example, when slaves prayed to a statue of the Virgin Mary, most were actually thinking of the African goddess of the sea, Lemanjá. Prayers to Xango, god of fire, thunder, and justice, were represented by the statue of Saint Jerome. This belief system came to be known by the general

This elaborate samba dance from a Brazilian Carnaval illustrates the over-the-top nature of the Carnaval celebrations before Lent.

name of macumba and included several sects. African drumming and singing were the driving force behind macumba rituals in which gods were drawn to earth through music in order to answer prayers.

As the population mixed musical and religious practices, both traditions remained alive. World music journalist Chris McGowan and Brazilian culture expert Ricardo Pessanha explain in *Brazilian Sound:*

> Sometimes slaves held drum sessions that on the surface seemed mere celebrations but in reality were religious rites. And, in turn . . . macumba helped preserve African musical characteristics. African songs, musical scales, musical instruments, and a rich variety of polyrhythms (each deity is called by a particular rhythm and song) have survived in their rituals.[21]

"To Dance with Joy"

During the course of several centuries, the sacred music of Africa was secularized into several forms. During the eighteenth century, a sensuous Angolan fertility dance called the lundu was adopted by members of Portuguese high society. The Portuguese modified the lundu by adding elements of the Spanish fandango. They Europeanized the music by adding refined harmonies along with piano and the Portuguese viola, a fretted guitar-like instrument. In this form, the lundu

Two worshipers honor the deities of macumba in a private home which also serves as a temple.

reigned as the most popular dance in Brazil until the early twentieth century. In 1889, an unnamed author described the lundu:

> The dancers are all seated or standing. A couple gets up and begins the festivity. At the beginning they hardly move; they snap their fingers with a noise like that of castanets, raise or arch their arms, and balance lazily. Little by little, the man becomes more animated: he performs revolutions around his partner, as if he were going to embrace her. She remains cold, disdains his advances; he redoubles his ardor. . . . She moves away, she leaps up; her movements become jerkier, she dances about in a passionate frenzy, while the viola (guitar) sighs and the enthusiastic spectators clap their hands.[22]

As the lundu moved to dance halls patronized by the upper classes, a rowdier music and dance style called the maxixe swept through the slums of Rio de Janeiro. The maxixe merged lundu music with the Brazilian tango, the habanera from Cuba, and the polka, introduced by touring French theater companies. Because it emerged in the steep hillside slums populated by ex-slaves, the maxixe was considered vulgar by Rio's ruling classes. In the early 1900s, parties and dance halls featuring maxixe music were targets for police repression. However, in the slum known as Praça Onze (Plaza Eleven), the maxixe was updated and combined with a style called the marcha, which was based on military marching music that featured a fast-tempo, one-two, one-two rhythm.

The merging of maxixe, marcha, and ancient bataque came to be known as samba, and the music followed two distinct paths. In fancy ballrooms, middle-class dancers embraced one another and swirled to the sounds of melodious samba-cancao. This style features sentimental lyrics sung with sophisticated harmonies and backed by stringed instruments, woodwinds, and percussion. In the streets, samba-enredo was riotous dance music played primarily on African percussion instruments such as the agogo, two metal bells hit with a stick; the single-headed atabaque drum; and the cuica, a small drum with a stick of bamboo inserted in the head. The cuica is played when the bamboo stick is rubbed with a wet cloth while the drummer manipulates the surrounding drumhead with his fingers. This action produces sounds similar to jungle birds, frogs, and howling monkeys.

Since it was first played in Rio, samba-enredo has emerged as the most popular form of samba. Its intricacies are described by McGowan and Pessanha:

> [Samba is] a vibrant musical form distinguished by increased [call-and-response] singing, more emphasis on percussive interplay, and

A raucous cuica drummer joins in the Carnaval party in Rio de Janeiro. The cuica can imitate jungle sounds.

a less formal sound than either maxixe or marcha. Technically, samba has a $2/4$ meter with its heaviest accent on the second beat . . . and many interlocking, syncopated lines in the melody and accompaniment. The main rhythm and abundant cross-rhythms can be carried by hand-clapping or in the percussion, which today may be performed by more than a dozen different drums and percussion instruments. Samba is commonly accompanied by the guitar and the four-stringed [ukulele-like] cavaquinho.[23]

In 1917, these elements came together in "On the Phone," the first samba ever recorded. The lyrics of the song say more about the style, perhaps, than any musical description: "The commandant of fun / Told me on the phone / To dance with joy."[24]

Carnaval Sambistas

By the time "On the Phone" was released, samba music and the rowdy spring festival of Carnaval were firmly linked. Although the roots of Carnaval can be traced back to the mid-1500s, the now-famed celebration of Brazil did not emerge until the early 1900s,

A typical Carnaval band and dancer perform in Rio. People from all over the world flock to Brazil during the spring festival.

when citizens of Rio held two pre-Lent carnivals. One Carnaval appealed to the upper classes, who formed elite groups called *sociedades* to organize dances and costume balls. The *sociedades* also held annual European-style parades featuring military brass bands, drum bands, and elaborately festooned carriages and floats. Rio's richest men and women attended the parades wearing cat and pig masks.

The mostly black and mulatto poor people, who were shut out of these festivities, initiated their own version of Carnaval, led by aggressive, all-male groups. These people paraded through the streets of the shantytowns dressed like African warriors. Musicians beat on African drums, and spectators sang the Carnaval anthem "Make Way" with lyrics that state: "Hey, make way / I want to pass / I like parties / I can't deny that."[25]

Individuals called *sambistas* who participated in the shantytown Carnaval were men who existed on the margins of society, often by illegal means. Their samba schools and samba societies, formed to organize and perpetuate their increasingly popular version of Carnaval, were often repressed and attacked by authorities.

Sambistas described their beleaguered lives with samba-enredo lyrics that addressed the discrimination and grinding poverty they faced every day. Songs described or made fun of street violence, prostitutes, and naive peasants from the country who were moving into the city slums. A favorite topic was the *malandro*, a street hustler who abhorred work but loved women, gambling, drinking, and partying. The 1931 song "Cool Mulatto" by Noel Rosa describes a typical *malandro*:

> This strong mulatto
> Is from Salgueiro
> Hanging around the dry cleaner's
> Was his favorite sport
> He was born lucky
> And since he was a kid
> He's lived from a pack of cards
> He's never seen a day's work.[26]

Although such lyrics were criticized by Rio's elites, they were extremely popular with average hardworking Brazilians, many of whom envied the lucky gambler in the song. Such songs also helped popularize the raucous version of Carnaval as practiced by the ex-slaves and their descendents.

When a new, more liberal, government took over Brazil in 1930, a policy of tolerance was enacted concerning the *sambistas*. Police no longer harassed samba societies, and the black Carnaval was officially considered *cultura afro-brasileira*, or part of Afro-Brazilian culture. The government was undoubtedly motivated by the fact that Carnaval was attracting an ever-growing number of tourists from around the world, giving the Brazilian economy a much-needed boost. Since that time, Carnaval has grown in scope and importance. Today, the four-day celebration in Rio is ten times bigger than its American counterpart, Mardi Gras in New Orleans. Other celebrations in

Songs of the Wicked *Malandra*

Samba writers often described the antics of lazy street hustlers called malandros. *The female version of the* malandro *is the* malandra. *Rejecting the traditional role of a stay-at-home wife and mother, the* malandra *refuses to cook, clean, or remain true to her mate. Instead, she makes her way in the world by betraying her lovers, flaunting her loose sexual morals, and bragging about a love of black magic and witchcraft. The 1927 "Shantytown Samba" by Sinho is a typical* malandra *samba:*

She fought all the time
But I did nothing to her
And she joined in the orgy
From dusk 'til dawn
And she told everybody
That she was free, that
    she was alone
She was the serpent's
    daughter
The cobra's granddaughter
I caught her swigging
    from a bottle
With the sorcerer
Making witchcraft
With my money
So I packed her bags for her
And sent them to her
To get her own back
She went off to live in the
    shantytown.

Quoted in Lisa Shaw, *A Social History of the Brazilian Samba*. Brookfield, VT: Ashgate, 1999, p. 17.

Salvador, Recife, and São Paulo are also attended by huge crowds.

Those who participate in Carnaval festivities attend samba schools that are found in every major city in Brazil. The schools, each with three to five thousand members, are formed by neighborhood groups and include citizens of all ages, from toddlers to senior citizens. Members of samba schools rehearse for Carnaval year round and hold weekly "samba nights" that are filled with dancing, singing, and band music. These important institutions also provide full-time employment to composers, musicians, and those who construct floats and sew costumes for the annual festival.

New and Old

The epicenter for Carnaval festivities is the massive seventy-thousand-seat, 766-yard-long (700-meter) stadium called the Sambadrome in Rio. During the last two days of Carnaval, attendees pay up to seven hundred dollars to watch dancers and drummers from dozens of samba schools stage eighty-minute-long parades, each featuring up to five thousand dancers, hundreds of drums, and a dozen magnificent floats, in an effort to win the title of Carnaval champion. The festivities are televised live and are seen by hundreds of millions of people worldwide.

Despite the ostentatious glamour of the modern Carnaval, many of Brazil's biggest stars remain true to their more humble roots. The popular singer Paulinho da Viola, for example, disdains digital keyboards and electric instruments for the traditional samba arrangements featuring guitar, cavaquinho, the tambourine-like pandeiro, and the tamborim, a small, high-pitched Brazilian drum.

Several best-selling women singers also celebrate the old with the new. For example, Clara Nunes is an enormously popular artist who has recorded more than sixteen albums of updated samba and pop songs. However, Nunes also sings songs that include religious invocations and lyrics steeped in macumba mythology.

Singer Beth Carvalho is known for her repertoire of catchy samba songs but also for her version of samba, known as pagode, that has a strong emphasis on African percussion. One of Carvalho's songs, "O Encanto do Gantois," is a tribute to the head priestess of a macumba sect in Salvador.

Alcione, another major female star in Brazil, explores many styles of samba, both old and new, as well as songs with indigenous roots. According to McGowan and Pessanha, she

Brazilian sambista Beth Carvalho gives a concert in France in 2005. Carvalho is known for her pagode style.

"can switch effortlessly between pop romantic ballads perfect for a dark . . . nightclub and folkloric excursions that would make an ethnomusicologist leap for his or her tape recorder and notebook."[27] Alcione, along with Carvalho and Nunes, are known as the three Queens of Samba, and their best-selling CDs are popular not only in Brazil but also in Europe, Japan, and the United States.

The New Beat of Bossa Nova

Modern samba artists are praised for their ability to combine new and old sounds in unique ways. Yet they are not the first to subject samba to original interpretations. In the late 1950s, singer-guitarist João Gilberto, a middle-class musician living in the Ipanema beach district of Rio, created a sensation with his version of samba called new beat, or bossa nova. Gilberto was inspired by what was called American cool jazz or West Coast jazz, made popular by artists such as saxophonist Gerry Mulligan and trumpet players Chet Baker and Shorty Rogers.

Gilberto created bossa nova by mellowing the samba rhythm into a laid-back style that could be played by fingerpicking a nylon-string guitar with no other instrumental accompaniment. He sang along to this beat in an exceptionally smooth, quiet vocal style. Gilberto's first recordings of the new sound, the songs "Chega de Saudade" and "Bim-Bom," were released in July 1958. Both featured calming, relaxed vocals and unusual harmonies considered off-key by some critics. Despite this view, the songs and a subsequent album by Gilberto kicked off a Brazilian bossa nova craze. Popular artists such as Sérgio Mendes and Lyra Leão were eager to capitalize on the fad by releasing albums of both new bossa nova songs and old samba songs played in the new style.

In 1964 bossa nova achieved spectacular success on the international scene when Gilberto teamed up with American jazz saxophonist Stan Getz for the Grammy-winning album *Getz/Gilberto*. A single from the album, "The Girl from Ipanema," sung by Gilberto in a bilingual duet with his wife, Astrud, became an international hit, selling over 2 million copies. "The Girl from Ipanema," with Astrud singing in English and João in Portuguese, was not planned, however. Astrud was in the studio simply to spend time with her husband. She was recruited to sing the vocal part on "Girl from Ipanema" only because João could not sing in English.

The *Getz/Gilberto* album inspired dozens of American jazz artists to merge the American and Brazilian styles. No longer a simple style with vocals and guitar, bossa nova was transformed by jazz players such as flutist Herbie Mann, saxophonist Paul Winter, and guitarist Charlie Byrd. Winter, who rose to fame playing bebop jazz, a form characterized by fast tempi and wild improvisation, comments on this phenomenon:

João Gilberto (left, on guitar) accompanies American jazz saxophonist Stan Getz onstage in 1972. Gilberto launched a bossa nova craze in the United States.

We were hearing a very gentle voice that had the kind of soul and harmonic beauty that we loved in jazz. But as opposed to the hard-driving bebop that we were playing then, it was astounding to find a very quiet, gentle music that had an equal amount of magic. It was a whole new possibility for us.[28]

Protest Music in Brazil

Whatever the possibilities of the music, in an era when the Beatles and other British rock bands were domi-

nating the airwaves, the bossa nova fad was over in the United States by 1965. In Brazil, however, the musical style was transformed once again as bossa nova and samba were combined with rock and roll and protest music called *Música Popular Brasileira*, or MPB.

MPB was not a specific style like bossa nova because it was interpreted differently by each artist. The songs did have common elements, however. MPB combined catchy melodies, vibrant harmonies, and Brazilian and rock rhythms with poetic lyrics that called for social justice. The style emerged at a time when a military coup had overthrown the progressive Brazilian government and replaced it with a repressive right-wing regime run by General Humberto Castelo Branco and a succession of brutal military dictators.

The MPB singers' style became nationally popular because of televised concerts. These shows featured fierce battles between performers who had to compete with about three thousand entrants before the top twelve were chosen for the televised match. The winners for best compositions, lyrics, musical arrangements, and traditional song interpretations might each receive about twenty thousand dollars.

The Jeers of the Audience

When MPB singers competed on popular television shows, they risked alienating their audiences with either mediocre songs or left-wing political views. Performer Sergio Ricardo did both in 1967, according to Christopher Dunn in Brutality Garden:

Sergio Ricardo, a well-known singer-songwriter associated with protest music . . . was initially well received by the audience, but his song "Beto bom de bola" (a song about the travails of a soccer player) failed to satisfy its expectations. On the last evening of the festival, the audience vocally rebuked the jury's selection of his song for the final round and jeered Ricardo when he appeared on stage. Unable to perform his song over the din, he hurled condescending remarks to the audience: "I would ask those who applaud and those who jeer to demonstrate *lucidez* [lucidity] at this moment in order to understand what I'm going to sing." His appeal to *lucidez* (a popular term among leftist intellectuals denoting the most proper ideological perspective) to legitimize his song and shame critics further provoked the ire of the audience. After a couple of false starts, he exclaimed: "You won. This is Brazil. This is an underdeveloped country! You're all a bunch of animals!" He proceeded to smash his guitar and hurl it at the audience, precipitating his disqualification from the festival.

Christopher Dunn, *Brutality Garden*. Chapel Hill: University of North Carolina Press, 2001, p. 64.

This was an astronomical sum at a time when the average Brazilian lived on only a few dollars a day. In addition, winners could record albums that might sell over one hundred thousand copies in a few weeks.

With names such as *Brazil Festival of Popular Music* and the *International Song Festival*, the TV shows became a national craze. On nights when the programs aired, streets, bars, and cafés were empty as millions stayed home to watch the musical battles. There was a political element to the competitions as well. When singers injected left-wing political content into their lyrics, those in the audience who supported the government waved flags and loudly booed and jeered them. Meanwhile, supporters tried to drown out the catcalls with loud cheers as singers tried to sing above the din.

Some of Brazil's most popular MPB singers were those who bravely opposed the government even though it was notorious for arresting, torturing, and killing dissidents. Singer-songwriter Geraldo Vandré, for example, consistently won competitions with angry lyrics that sympathized with the plight of repressed farmers, workers, and left-wing students. The songs Vandré performed on MPB television shows between 1966 and 1968 also drew the attention of officials, who called his lyrics subversive, offensive to the military, and supportive of illegal student demonstrators. Fearing for his life, the popular singer was forced to leave Brazil in 1969.

Right-wing government supporters also interfered with the popular poet, musician, and playwright Chico Buarque. When a play featuring his songs was staged in Rio in 1968, a group of armed militants invaded the theater and beat up actors, technicians, and Buarque himself. Weeks later, the government instituted strict censorship of all the arts. Hundreds of singers, musicians, and intellectuals disappeared into the country's prisons and were never seen again.

Tropicalia

Even as some MPB musicians were facing intense pressure from the government, another school of Brazilian music arose that was considered even more radical by authorities. The style, called tropicalia, was a popular music form forged among artists, intellectuals, workers, politicians, and activists who opposed the tactics of Castelo Branco and his administration. The tropicalia movement coalesced around singers who were saddened by the widespread misery they saw around them. Christopher Dunn, codirector of the Brazilian Studies Council at Tulane University, explains in *Brutality Garden*:

> Tropicália was both a mournful critique of [the political] defeats as well as an exuberant, if often ironic, celebration of Brazilian culture and its continuous permutations. As its name suggests, the movement referenced Brazil's

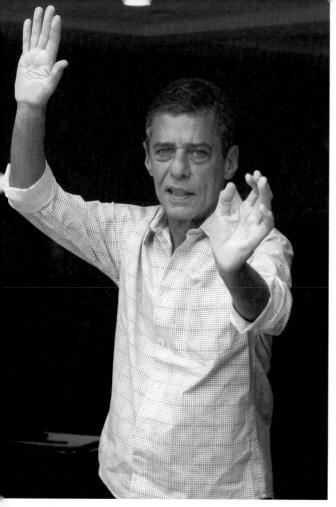

Liberal artist Chico Buarque was beaten for voicing opposition to the repressive, right-wing Brazilian government.

and social misery. The juxtaposition of tropical plenitude and state repression is best captured in the phrase . . . "brutality garden" which was taken from a key tropicalist song.[29]

Like MPB, tropicalia was first played to a national audience on a televised music competition. In 1967 Caetano Veloso and Gilberto Gil introduced the style, playing songs that mixed bossa nova, rock and roll, Brazilian folk music, African music, and Portuguese fado. Many Brazilians disliked this musical amalgamation intensely because rock and roll and electric guitars were disdained by the public in the land of the samba. Despite the passionate criticism, however, tropicalists took glee in offending the public. In 1968, though, Veloso went too far. Appearing at the International Song Festival in plastic clothes with his band the Mutants, Veloso was unable to finish his song "Forbidding is Forbidden" because of the raucous booing. Gil faced worse problems. In 1969 his songs so irritated Brazil's dictator that he was jailed for a time without ever being charged with a crime. Veloso was also imprisoned for several months in 1969, charged with antigovernment activities. The performer was forced into exile in London upon his release.

The tropicalia movement, which encompassed music, film, theater, poetry,

tropical climate, which throughout history has been exalted for generating lush abundance or lamented for impeding economic development along the line of societies located in temperate climates. The tropicalists purposefully invoked stereotypical images of Brazil as a tropical paradise only to subvert them with pointed references to political violence and avant-garde art, was brief, lasting only from 1967 to 1969. However, the freedom to experiment exhibited by its musical practitioners opened up doors for other musicians, who began combining rock with traditional Brazilian music. By the mid-1970s, the novel styles that incited violent booing in the 1960s had become part of mainstream Brazilian music. Gil himself continued to experiment, drawing heavily from African music such as juju as well as reggae and funk.

Veloso, too, continued to innovate after he returned to Brazil in 1972. In the 1980s he began drawing on reggae, samba, and frevo from northern Brazil for inspiration. By the 1990s, Veloso and Gil were both major stars in Brazil, along with other former tropicalists such as Gal Costa, Maria Bethânia, João Bosco, and Milton Nascimento.

Their music influenced a new generation of musicians in the United States. Rock stars Beck, Nelly Furtado, David Byrne, and Kurt Cobain of Nirvana have all cited tropicalia as a major influence. In 1998, Beck named his new album, *Mutations*, as a tribute to Veloso's Mutants. One single from the album, "Tropicalia," reached number twenty-one on *Billboard*'s modern rock singles chart.

Tropical Rock and Rap

The tropicalists also inspired rock musicians in Brazil to make tropical rock that combines American, English, and Brazilian influences. Overcoming prejudices against Americanized music,

Innovative Brazilian singer-songwriter Caetano Veloso helped develop the tropicalia style. Although brief, the tropicalia movement paved the way for further musical experimentation in Brazil.

Brazilian Hip-Hop

Brazilian rap is often blended with other musical forms, such as samba, reggae, soul, acid-jazz, and bossa nova. The following article by Angel Romero, "The Rough Guide to Brazilian Hip-Hop, a New Wave of Talent," describes some of the top acts in Brazil's hip-hop scene:

"Sou Negrão" is a Brazilian rap classic performed by Rappin' Hood and Johnny MC of PosseMente Zulu—one of the most important rap bands in Brazil. . . . The principal exponent of the manguebeat movement, Chico Science has participated in various bands that have incorporated soul, funk and hip-hop. . . .

Dexter and Afro-X created [the song] "509-E" (their cell number in Carandiru prison) after being imprisoned and condemned to ten years for armed assault. Both of them are originally from Vila Calux, a violent area in São Bernardo Do Campo on the outskirts of São Paulo, and "Saudades Mil," from their debut album, takes the format of a letter that Dexter is writing to a girlfriend. . . .

Weapons, prisons and violence are the usual themes covered by local rap music. However, some artists such as Somos Nós A Justiça ("We Are The Law") see rap music as a means of discussing issues such as social inequality, race and poverty. . . . Stereo Maracaña was created in 1999 by Pedro D-Lita and Maurício Pacheco, who believe that through their musical repertoire they can inspire their listeners to appreciate the day-to-day realities of people who are constantly struggling for the basic rights of food, work, decent housing and healthcare.

Angel Romero, "The Rough Guide to Brazilian Hip-Hop, a New Wave of Talent," World Music Central, September 7, 2005. www.worldmusiccentral.org/article.php?story=20040907093802703.

Brazilian tropical rockers today play in various styles that include punk, heavy metal, folk rock, and pop.

Brazilian rock began to boom in the 1980s, and the music received a huge boost from the Rock in Rio festival, first held in 1985. The week-long event, attended by a total of 1.4 million people and broadcast on national TV, featured international acts such as Queen as well as Brazilian acts, including Gil and rocker Rita Lee. In 2001, Rock in Rio was broadcast in fifty countries. The 2004 version of the festival was even larger, drawing nearly 1.5 million rock fans who came to hear Britney Spears as well as Brazilian rockers João Pedro Pais and Fattiqueira.

Rap music has also been a growing trend in Brazil since the 1990s, driven by the popularity of Os Racionais MCs. As Jan Field, founder of the Brazilian arts and culture magazine *Caos*, writes, Os Racionais MCs "made their name by performing relentlessly in the [barrio] and rapping about drug-trafficking, racism, and government corruption. Hard-hitting street beats heavy on drums and bass—inspired by old-school North American rappers like Run-DMC and Public Enemy—back samples and loops of Brazilian popular music."[30] In 1998, Os Racionais MCs' album *Sobrevivendo no Inferno* (Surviving in Hell) sold over a million copies, a record number of sales for independent releases in Brazil. The video received the Viewer's Choice Award from MTV Brazil as well as the Video of the Year Award.

From the ancient bataque through samba, MBP, and tropical rock and rap, Brazil's music scene has seen constant change even as the old musical styles have endured. In a nation where music and dance are central to daily life, there is little doubt that the music of Brazil will continue to merge, mutate, and explode onto the airwaves from South America to North America, Europe, and beyond.

Chapter Four

Music of South America

T he Brazilian samba and bossa nova tend to overshadow musical styles from other South American countries. However, all South American nations have rich musical histories, and each country has its own unique styles of music. Like the samba in Brazil, these styles developed with varying degrees of influences from Amerindian, African, and European cultures.

Musicologists divide South America into three zones of cultural influence. The nations of Argentina, Chile, and Uruguay have a dominant Spanish European culture. Bolivia, Paraguay, Ecuador, and parts of Colombia and Venezuela exhibit strong Amerindian influences. The coastal regions tend to have the largest cities and so contain a dominant black influence in the working-class areas, often mixed with a Spanish element around government centers.

Cumbia from Colombia

Colombia is a good example of the complex musical geography of South America. The nation is divided into several separate regions, each producing distinct musical styles that evolved from their own unique cultural influences. Indigenous music dominates the nation's interior rain forests, where Amerindians moved to escape Spanish conquest. Interior valleys contain regions where African influence is strongest as a result of settlement by runaway slaves. Meanwhile, along the coasts, Spanish influence and power remained strong.

As in most other South American nations, music influenced by African rhythms and melodies has remained the most popular style throughout the country. Foremost among these styles is the cumbia, a drum-based music and dance style modeled on the cumbe from Guinea, where the word means "celebration."

The roots of the cumbia can be traced to the late 1600s, when African and Amerindian slaves gathered to dance and play music on holidays. During those times, the streets filled with men and women dressed in white. The women wore long, layered skirts, and the men wore red neckerchiefs and carried bundles of flaming white candles.

The cumbia celebration began as the celebrants formed a large circle. Drummers played complex layered beats featuring three African drums, the llamador, alegro, and bombo or tambora. Women danced flirtatiously in the middle of the circle, enticing the men to draw close and then pushing them away as they advanced. As the volume and intensity of the drumming increased, the men tried to outdo one another, performing increasingly difficult dance moves to win the women's attention. The candles were passed one by one to the females as symbolic floral bouquets.

In later centuries, the cumbia sound changed as it merged with Spanish lyrical song structures and the wistful melodies of Amerindian ballads. Over time, Colombians added new instruments to the traditional African drum and voice arrangements. Those with Amerindian back-

grounds added scrapers, cane flutes, and the gaita, a long, sharp-toned flute. Those with Spanish roots played cumbia on guitars and lutelike ouds. European band instruments such as trombones, clarinets, saxophones,

A Colombian musician plays cumbia music on a traditional flute. The cumbia style is popular throughout Latin America.

trumpets, and accordions were also brought to the mix. Throughout this musical evolution, the cumbia retained the sexual nature of the original dance as macho singers called parranderos, or partying men, sang lyrics boasting of their conquests.

As cumbia music grew in popularity, the African rhythms, melodies, and dances associated with the style spread to other nations. In Venezuela, for example, a different style of cumbia is played during feasts celebrating Saint John the Baptist.

A Rolling Infectious Beat

Although the cumbia's origins are in Guinea, the music has a strong Amerindian influence, unlike other South American styles such as the samba and mambo. Morales describes the one-two, one-two cumbia beat, often likened to riding a horse at a loping trot:

> In essential elements, the [tambora] drums and enormous gaita flutes, combine to give the music a rolling infectious . . . beat that seems like a fusion between merengue and reggae, with a similar back beat that sends it surging forward. . . . The cumbia tempo stresses the upbeat, allowing the cumbia to "float" and giving it a kind of perpetual optimistic lift.[31]

Although the beat remained the same, the place of the cumbia in Colombian society continued to change. In the early centuries, the style was considered vulgar and crude, music for slave dances that was shunned by the descendents of the European ruling class. In 1820, however, as Colombia struggled for independence from Spain, the cumbia came to symbolize liberty, freedom, and the fight against colonialism. By the early years of the twentieth century, cumbia was widely celebrated as the national sound of Colombia.

In the late 1940s, as the Cuban mambo and cha-cha-cha fads were taking New York by storm, Colombian musicians began immigrating to the United States to play cumbia to American audiences. In New York, the sound quickly merged with the Afro-Cuban and Puerto Rican influences that eventually led to salsa in the 1970s.

In Colombia the 1950s were known as the Golden Age of Cumbia as the sound blended with mambo and big band jazz influences. During this time, a bandleader named Fruko founded a record company, Disco Fuentes, that successfully promoted cumbia artists and records throughout Latin America. One of Fruko's acts, La Sonora Dinamita, was responsible for popularizing cumbia in Mexico in the 1960s. In the years that followed, the "mother of Colombian rhythms"[32] attracted millions of fans throughout Latin America, with local styles emerging in Panama, El Salvador, Chile, Bolivia, Ecuador, and elsewhere.

In the twenty-first century, cumbia is strongly influenced by the MTV

A couple dance the mambo in 1958. Derived from Cuban cha-cha-cha, the mambo became a dance sensation in the United States.

rock-and-roll generation. The group Ivan y sus Bam Band draws on particular musical and visual styles to attract young fans. Their performances feature four scantily clad female dancers, a drum machine pounding out a heavy beat, and a large brass section playing cumbia rhythms.

In an even newer incarnation, musicians have added computerized beats and sound effects to the cumbia sound to produce techno-cumbia. This digitized sound is popular in Latin dance clubs throughout the world.

Tango Takes Off

The cumbia is one of many Latin American music and dance styles that emerged among the continent's poorest and most downtrodden citizens. In Buenos Aires, Argentina, the impoverished inhabitants of the city's treacherous slums invented the tango in the latter part of the nineteenth century. This dance later traveled around the globe and generated one of the most popular musical fads of the twentieth century.

In the 1880s Buenos Aires was a melting pot of former black slaves,

Dancing the Redondo in Venezuela

In Venezuela, people of African descent who live in the state of Yaracuy celebrate their patron saint, John the Baptist, with a dance similar to the Colombian cumbia. It is described by Max H. Brandt in The Garland Handbook of Latin American Music:

During the feast of Saint John the Baptist . . . a dance requires many people to participate at the same time, usually multiple pairs or three or more people dancing in a line or a circle, each with an arm or a hand on his or her neighbor's shoulder. The redondos [round drums] accompany a standard song and dance performed by one male-female couple at a time, the person of each gender being alternately replaced by someone from the audience. A man and a woman dance provocatively in circular movements as spectators form a circular arena around them. The dancers' movements and the formation of the onlookers . . . are said to give this drum and its music the name redondo "round."

A rhythm and song known as *malembe* accompanies the street processions with the image of Saint John the Baptist. Minas [a type of drum] or redondos accompany the malembes and processions with a unison rhythm. . . . Though malembe means "softly, slowly, take it easy" in various Bantu languages, the people . . . are not aware of its African roots and use it simply as the name of a kind of music.

Quoted in Dale A. Olsen and Daniel E. Sheehy, eds., *The Garland Handbook of Latin American Music*. New York: Garland, 2000, p. 239.

white South Americans, European and Caribbean immigrants, and recently arrived rural Amerindians. The musical influences heard in the city were as diverse as its population. Sounds of flamenco from southern Spain mingled in the streets with Italian accordion melodies, syncopated African and Cuban habanera rhythms, European mazurkas and polkas, and the lonely country songs of Argentine gauchos, or cowboys.

Buenos Aires was a boomtown, and most of the population was male. This spawned an underworld of cheap bars and seedy brothels. In the early years of the twentieth century, men who lacked female partners practiced dancing with one another. The dances often degenerated into violent competitions with macho, knife-wielding dancers engaging in mock battle. In brothels, the tango took on an air of sexual possession as men danced cheek-to-cheek with prostitutes.

The music of the tango was played on inexpensive instruments, including flutes, guitars, violins, and a concertina-like instrument called a bandoneon. In later years, tango bands grew in size to include the double bass, piano, and several violins and bandoneons.

Considered scandalous and immoral by polite society, the tango remained unknown outside Buenos Aires until an upper-class Argentine writer, Ricardo Güiraldes, described the dance in the 1911 poem "Tango." He wrote that the tango was like the "all-absorbing love of a tyrant, jealously guarding his dominion over women who have surrendered submissively, like obedient beasts."[33] This shocking description helped popularize the tango among the decadent upper

This Argentine couple shows off their tango skills. Originating in the seedy parts of Buenos Aires, the provocative dance is popular throughout the world.

classes in Argentine society. In 1912, Güiraldes traveled to Paris, where he thrilled high society with lurid tango demonstrations.

The tango fad soon spread to the United States, where the dance was condemned by politicians and the clergy, celebrated in the press, and taught to eager students in hundreds of ballrooms up and down the East Coast. In 1914, New York City rabbi Abraham Wise summed up the general attitude of religious authorities toward the tango: "If one were to enter a New York ballroom after a ten years' absence, one would be struck dumb and speechless at the degeneration which has come to pass."[34]

Official scorn did little to quell the fad, however, and between 1920 and 1945, tango was a driving force in the entertainment business. Argentine bandleader Roberto Firpo and singer Carlos Gardél sold hundreds of thousands of records and filled ballrooms in Europe, South America, and the United States. Hollywood helped sell the tango trend with several films in which America's biggest movie star, Rudolph Valentino, performed the dance.

Tango rhythms were drowned out by rock and roll in the 1950s. However, the style evolved into the nuevo, or new, tango in the 1960s when bandoneon player Astor Piazolla added jazz chord structures and rhythms. Since the 1990s Argentine musicians have melded the most up-to-date elements to the style, using digital instruments to produce neo-tango records

with complex polyrhythms and intricate melodies. And perhaps to prove that everything old can become new again, dance halls featuring the original style of tango are attracting a new generation of fans who are enamored with the dance's rich history and often wicked nature.

The Argentine Beatles

Millions of Argentines continue to dance the tango, but the nation has also produced its share of rock-and-roll bands. Beginning in the 1950s, groups such as Los Shakers and Los Beatniks introduced rock music to young dancers in Buenos Aires. Rock audiences remained small, however, until the early 1970s, when pianist and composer Charly Garcia injected a creative and controversial element into rock music.

Garcia was a child prodigy pianist who grew up in a wealthy family in Buenos Aires. Like millions of others who came of age in the 1960s, Garcia was heavily influenced by the Beatles. The Beatles broke up in 1970, but Garcia was inspired to form his own Beatlesque rock band, Sui Generis, in 1972. The group's first album, *Vida*, sold eighty thousand copies, a large number for an unknown band in a nation where most people detested rock and roll.

Calling himself the Third World John Lennon, after the outspoken singer-songwriter in the Beatles, Garcia used his band to push the boundaries of acceptable lyrical content while drawing on his life experiences

Born to Sing Tango

Carlos Gardél is a national hero in Argentina, where he is revered for his contributions to tango music between 1920 and 1935. His story is told by Teddy Peiro and Jan Fairley in World Music: Latin and North America, Caribbean, India, Asia and Pacific:

The extraordinary figure of Carlos Gardél was—and still is—a legend in Argentina, and he was a huge influence in spreading the popularity of tango round the world. In Argentina, it was Gardél above all who transformed tango from an essentially low-down dance form to a song style popular among Argentines of widely differing social classes. His career coincided with the first period of tango's Golden Age and the development of *tango-canción* (tango song) in the 1920s and '30s. The advent of radio, recording and film all helped his career, but nothing helped him more than his own voice—a voice that was born to sing tango and which became the model for all future singers of the genre. . . .

Everything about Gardél, his voice, his image, his suavity, his posture, his arrogance and his natural machismo spelled tango.

. . . During his career, Gardél recorded some nine hundred songs and starred in numerous films, notably *The Tango on Broadway* in 1933. He was tragically killed in an air crash in Colombia at the height of his fame, and his legendary status was confirmed. His image is still everywhere in Buenos Aires, on plaques and huge murals, and in record store windows, while admirers pay homage to his life-sized, bronze statue in the Chacarita cemetery, placing a lighted cigarette between his fingers or a red carnation in his buttonhole.

Quoted in Simon Broughton and Mark Ellingham, eds., *World Music, Latin and North America, Caribbean, India, Asia and Pacific.* London: Rough Guides, 2000, p. 307.

The embodiment of Argentine tango, the glamorous Carlos Gardél sings in a radio studio in the 1930s.

for inspiration. For example, after he was drafted at the age of twenty, the singer took a large dose of amphetamines and faked a heart attack in order to get expelled from military service. While recovering, he wrote two songs about the experience, "Crazy Boots," about the military, and "Song for My Death," about his drug overdose.

Garcia's next album, *Little Anecdotes About the Institutions*, contained the two controversial songs, along with the antigovernment "John Repression." These songs, however, were censored by the government, and the lyrics of another song about censorship itself, "Who Am I Singing For, Then?" also had to be changed.

Garcia quit Sui Generis in 1975 but continued to write controversial lyrics that he put to experimental music. In 1979, he was called into a meeting with Eduardo Harguindeguy, the Argentine security minister secretly referred to as the Devil by political resisters. The government official warned Garcia that if he did not change the political tone of his lyrics, he would be imprisoned. Fearing arrest, Garcia hid his political commentary in abstract lyrics on the 1980 album *Bicycle*, recorded with his new group, Serú Girán. One track, "Song of Alice in (Wonder) Land" referenced characters from the Lewis Carroll story to criticize the Argentine military government. Another song, "Meeting with the Devil," slyly referred to Harguindeguy's warning. *Bicycle* was a huge success, and the press and public

began calling Serú Girán the Argentine Beatles.

Despite the success of Serú Girán's five albums, Garcia left the band and started a solo career in 1982. In the years that followed, he experimented with punk rock, conceptual music, and songs heavily influenced by cocaine, whiskey, and other drugs. Although his career had many ups and downs, by 2005, Garcia had released seventy-one albums and was considered one of the most talented and influential figures of Argentine and Latin rock.

Garcia's impact has been felt across the entire rock spectrum in Argentina and has been a major influence on a new generation of rock stars, including Fito Paez, Soda Stereo, and Los Fabulosos Cadillacs, who drew upon political events and personal misfortunes for lyrical inspiration. Like Garcia, these acts are unafraid to mix musical styles as diverse as funk, ska, reggae, and acid rock.

Songs of Resistance

Authorities in Argentina well understood the power of music to rally the public against government policies. In retaliation, they silenced musicians with threats of arrest. In nations such as Chile, authorities did more than pressure musicians to change their lyrical content. Those who committed the crime of criticizing the dictators in song were imprisoned, tortured, and killed.

Despite such repressive measures, musicians who put their grievances

The controversial Charly Garcia sings with his guitar in Peru in 2001. Garcia's early work was heavily influenced by the Beatles.

into verse and melody were following an old Latin American tradition in which folk songs guardedly poked fun at those in power or criticized the status quo. In the 1960s, however, a type of music, nueva cancion, or new song, dispensed with subtlety and openly questioned the legitimacy of the government.

Nueva cancion, most often associated with Chile, actually began in Argentina as a reaction to the dominance of tango in the national culture. The first nueva cancion singers were simply interested in reviving the songs played by downtrodden farmers and workers who were said to preserve admirable traditions of music and culture. Nueva cancion songs, therefore, expressed feelings of antimaterialism and antimodernism and focused on the thoughts and emotions of average citizens.

When the new song movement was adopted in Chile, singers felt that it was their obligation to influence the politics of the country to improve the lives of working people. This meant writing songs critical of the small group of corrupt Chilean military authorities who controlled nearly all the wealth. In this unequal society, the populace was purposely denied educational opportunities and economic advancement. Jan Fairley, a journalist who specializes in Latin American music, describes the response of the new song artists to this situation in *World Music: Latin and North America, Caribbean, India, Asia and Pacific*:

> With voice and guitar, they composed songs for their own hopes and experiences in places where many of those involved in the struggles for change regularly met and socialized. It is a music that . . . [used the] guitar as gun and song as bullet. Yet the songs—poems written to be performed—are classic expressions of the years of hope and the struggle for change, and their beauty and truth nurtured those suffering under dictatorship or forced into exile. They are still known by heart by audiences throughout the continent and its exile communities.[35]

The first well-known nueva cancion artist in Chile was Violeta Parra, born in 1917. Her early musical career was

This quena player in native dress provides music at a Bolivian feast. Nueva cancion music has its roots in Amerindian folk songs.

based on playing traditional Chilean songs. In the 1950s, she began traveling through the countryside seeking out unrecorded folk songs composed by *payadores*, rural Amerindian poets who followed ancient musical traditions. Parra played the collected songs on radio shows and began to write lyrics similar to those she heard from the *payadores*. These songs served as the foundation of the nueva cancion movement. Parra not only appreciated the poetry of Amerindians, but she was also the first to popularize their instruments on the radio. Her backup band used a bamboo flute, or quena, and a small, ten-string lute with a body made from an armadillo shell.

Despite her musical success, Parra suffered from depression, and she committed suicide in 1967. Her music has lived on, however. Her whimsical song "Thanks to Life" was covered by American folk singer Joan Baez and many others.

"No Revolution Without Song"

The nueva cancion style performed by Parra came at a time when millions of Chileans were striving to replace their repressive government with democratically elected officials. In 1965, the center for this movement in Santiago was the folk club Peña de los Parra, opened by Parra's children, Angel and Isabel. The club served as a meeting place where activists could hear the music of the popular nueva cancion musician Victor Jara, who often played with and was greatly influenced by Parra.

Jara himself had sterling credentials to sing nueva cancion. He grew up in the squalid shantytown outside of Santiago and survived by helping his mother sell food from a tiny stall downtown. Jara created controversy beginning with his first public performances. One song charged the minister of the interior with ordering the slaughter of impoverished farmers in southern Chile. Other Jara songs were drawn from the singer's own experiences and focused on the harsh details of life, death, and lost love in Santiago's shantytown.

Jara was extremely popular, and his music was at the forefront of democratic change in Chile. In the late 1960s, the singer was a driving force behind the Popular Unity Party, whose candidate, Salvador Allende, was elected president of Chile in 1970. At a celebratory concert in Santiago, Jara appeared onstage with Allende and other nueva cancion musicians under a banner that read: "There Can Be No Revolution Without Song."[36]

The Allende revolution did not last long, however. On September 11, 1973, Allende was murdered during a coup d'état. The military dictatorship of Augusto Pinochet took over the government, and five thousand people formerly associated with Allende, including Jara, were arrested and taken to a downtown soccer stadium. Later, Jara was taken to jail. There, he wrote the words to the haunting poem "Chile Stadium," which reads in part:

There are five thousand of us here
in this little part of the city. . . .
How much humanity
exposed to hunger, cold, panic,
    pain,
moral pressures, terror and
    insanity?
What horror the face of fascism
    creates!
How hard it is to sing
when I must sing of horror.
Horror which I am living.
Horror which I am dying. . . .
in which silence and screams. . . .[37]

The next day, Jara was taken back to the stadium, where soldiers used rifle butts to break his wrists and hands. Finally, he was shot with a machine gun. His bullet-riddled body was dumped with dozens of others near a local cemetery, and a mortuary worker who recognized him reported his death.

After Jara's demise, the Pinochet government worked to repress the new song movement. Jara's records and those of others were confiscated, and the music was banned from the radio. Anyone caught playing or listening to

A man outside Chile Stadium, renamed Victor Jara Stadium in 2003, mourns the deaths of political prisoners. Musician Jara was murdered inside the stadium in 1973.

Los Fabulosos Cadillacs

The rock band Los Fabulosos Cadillacs, from Buenos Aires, Argentina, formed in 1985. Since that time, their eclectic brand of music has attracted fans throughout South and Central America, the United States, and Great Britain. The band has won several Grammy Awards, and they have played with some of the biggest stars in the music business. The following biography of the band was written by Sandra Brennan for the Music Match Web site:

The internationally renowned and versatile Argentine band Los Fabulosos Cadillacs have been thrilling audiences with their eclectic mixture of rock, rap, ska, reggae, and traditional South American sounds. . . . The nine piece band began in 1985 and chose the name Los Fabulosos Cadillacs only because they thought it sounded good. Then as . . . now, the band is run democratically and there is no one leader; they play whatever style most appeals to them at the moment and each of their ten albums is different from the last. In 1995, they recorded the album *Rey Azucar . . .* [that] featured guest appearances from Debbie Harry [of Blondie] and from Mick Jones, the ex-guitarist from the Clash. According to the band members, working with Jones was a dream come true. One of their biggest commercial hits in South America is "Matador" which, with its up-tempo samba-reggae inspired beat, appeared as a bonus track on their 1995 greatest hits album *Vasos Vacios*. The Cadillacs have extensively toured Latin America and in 1995, appeared in Anaheim, California, where they knocked 'em dead with their lively performance. Though the band was in a slump during the early '90s, their greatest hits album revitalized their career. *Marcha del Golazo Solitario* followed in 1999 and two live albums, *Hola* and *Chau*, were issued in early 2001.

Sandra Brennan, "Los Fabulosos Cadillacs," Music Match, 2001. www.mmguide.musicmatch.com/artist/artist.cgi?ARTISTID=351361&TMPL=LONG #bio.

nueva cancion could be arrested, tortured, or killed. Despite these measures, however, nueva cancion survived.

Pinochet was removed from office in 1990, making the political style of nueva cancion no longer necessary. Yet the use of traditional instruments and socially relevant lyrics remains popular in Chile and elsewhere. Jara has become a musical legend, and his songs have been recorded by folk singer Pete Seeger as well as rock musicians Jackson Browne, Peter Gabriel, Bruce Springsteen, and Sting. And old nueva cancion from the 1960s and 1970s are considered by some to be nearly as important as Chile's national anthem.

From Chile to Colombia and throughout South America, homegrown music has acted as a wellspring of hope, culture, love of nation, and romance. Whether it was used to dance the night away or challenge a deadly dictator, African, European, and Amerindian song has helped write the history of a large and diverse continent.

Chapter Five

Mexican Music in Two Nations

Until the sixteenth century, the music of Mexico was played by Aztec and Maya musicians. When their society was colonized by the Spanish, elements of their musically advanced sounds remained alive among their descendents. Today about three-quarters of Mexicans are mestizos—people of mixed European and Native American ancestry—and the musical roots of the indigenous Mesoamericans can be heard in Mexican styles ranging from folk songs to techno-banda and hip-hop.

Each Mexican region has its own unique blend of cultural influences. In southern Mexico, traditional music has a strong Amerindian flavor, while in the central regions, European harps are played with African rhythms. Musicians in northern Mexico and the U.S. border areas play a cornucopia of styles, with Spanish martial horns influencing mariachi and banda music, European polkas driving norteño, and

American pop and rock and roll spicing Tejano and other forms. As Dale A. Olsen and mariachi musician Daniel E. Sheehy write in *The Garland Handbook of Latin American Music:* "[Modern] descendents of ancient Amerindian cultures, rural-rooted mestizo traditions, African-derived traits, and international urban popular music exist side-by-side, giving rise to new musical hybrids."[38]

This musical fusion thrives in Mexico thanks to a large, influential community of young people who dictate musical tastes not only for the entire nation but all of Central America. Mexican listeners also support a burgeoning entertainment industry that promotes the products of the music business on television and radio. In addition, the border that Mexico shares with the United States has allowed people and musical ideas to flow freely between Mexico, California, Texas, and other American states.

Son Songs in Mexico

While modern Mexican music has a variety of influences, its roots are in the son style that is derived from an amalgamation of Spanish, African, and Amerindian elements. However, the Mexican form developed independently from Cuban music of the same name, and each has its own unique forms today.

There are eight different styles of Mexican son, some more popular than others. Although the musical forms are different, they all developed in rural areas, where audiences participated in foot-stamp dancing, or zapateado.

When performing the zapateado, participants drive the heels of their shoes and boots into the dance floor, pounding out a fast counter rhythm to the musical beat in a way that adds tension and excitement to the music. One of the most famous zapateados is the jarabe tapatio, or Mexican hat dance, from Guadalajara, Jalisco. This dance, in which men wear the costumes of the Jalisco cowboy, or *charro*, and the women wear handwoven shawls and colorful sequined skirts, is the national dance of Mexico.

Son audiences help shape the lyrical makeup of songs. As vocalists

Mariachis in their charro suits play music for the lively Mexican hat dance, a famous example of zapateado.

sing, audience members shout out comments from the dance floor. Singers are expected to respond immediately with clever and amusing lyrics, and those who fail are jeered. Musicians depend on this interaction, adding fanciful runs or flourishes on the violin or guitar to accompany the improvised lyrics.

Individual son styles are defined by their instrumentation and musical traditions. For example, some son jarocho from Veracruz features a thirty-two-string harp that plays a melody; a shallow-bodied guitar called a jarana, used to strum rhythmic chords; and a small, four-stringed guitar called a requinto, on which improvised riffs are played. In southern Veracruz, where harps are not common, a different style of son jarocho features guitars of various sizes along with the pandero, an eight-sided drum with small metal jingles like a tambourine.

Another form of son originated among the Zapotec Indians in Oaxaca. Called son istmenos, it features romantic lyrics and is played in a slow, melancholy 3/4 waltz time. The haunting istmenos songs of love and loss have been adapted by non-Indian singers who have learned the Zapotec language to add authenticity to their renditions. One of the most popular urban vocalists in this style is Lila Downs, who is half Amerindian and half American.

Still another form of son, arribeno, is especially beloved by country people in the rural regions of central Mexico. It is played by *trovadores*, or troubadours, who improvise lyrics about poverty, politics, and the difficulties of making a living from the land. When performing, the musicians compete with one another, as Latin American music scholar Mary Farquharson describes it in *World Music:*

> Two trovadores, each playing the huapanguera [a large, eight-string guitar] and each accompanied by two violins and the small *vihuela* [five-string] guitar, confront each other on tall bamboo platforms erected on the sides of a village square. According to an established structure, they enter into musical combat, improvising verses which are interspersed with zapateado dancing.[39]

Mariachi from Jalisco

The most popular form of son is mariachi music. It is also called sones jaliscienses, meaning sons from Jalisco, the state where the music originated in the mid-nineteenth century. Mariachi bands can have up to twenty players, but all feature at least two violins, two trumpets, one Spanish guitar, one vihuela, and a guitarron (a jumbo acoustic bass guitar).

Mariachi music was originally played at weddings, and some say the name is a corruption of the French word for marriage. The music moved beyond wedding celebrations in the early twentieth century when unemployed musicians tried to earn a living traveling from village to village to sing songs about love affairs, revolutionary heroes, and current events.

In the 1930s mariachi became the national sound of Mexico when it was popularized by radio stations and record companies. Movies were responsible for making mariachi popular throughout the world. In the 1940s and 1950s, the golden age of mariachi, the band Vargas de Tecalitlán appeared in over two hundred Mexican films shown throughout Latin America. North of the border in Hollywood, the band Mariachi Vargas was featured in dozens of movies. This band, said to be among the best of the mariachi bands, is still playing today. Although the original players have all died, the personnel of the band is constantly updated with Mexico's most talented musicians.

Beating Harps and Dancing Horses

There are many unique, localized versions of Mexican son music, but one of the most unusual comes from the Michoacán region. In this area, which is called "Hell's Waiting Room" because of its hot climate, local people enjoy sones de arpa grande, or son of the big harp. Bands that play this style feature two guitars, two violins, and one big harp. The performance style is described by Mary Farquharson in World Music: Latin and North America, Caribbean, Indian, Asia and Pacific*:*

The style involves the sound boxes of the big harps being beaten in counter-rhythm by one of the musicians of the band, or by a local fan who pays for the privilege. The harpist, meanwhile, must hold on to the melody—and his harp—delivering a vocal line that can sound something like a shout from the soul.

This style of son used to thrive at country fairs and urban brothels, but today, the audiences are the locals who organize parties on the small farms far from the city, or wealthy stable-owners who pride themselves on their dancing horses. The horses will apparently only dance to the big harp music and they do so on wooden platforms, beating out rhythm and counter-rhythm with their hooves.

Quoted in Simon Broughton and Mark Ellingham, eds., *World Music: Latin and North America, Caribbean, India, Asia and Pacific*. London: Rough Guides, 2000, p. 468.

Ranchera Country

Mariachi singers often sing popular songs in the ranchera style. Ranchera first emerged in the 1930s, when millions of Mexican peasants moved from rural areas to large cities. These people were forced off the land by economic hardship, and they often grew nostalgic for country life as they struggled to survive in Mexico City, Tijuana, and elsewhere. Ranchera singers responded by writing country songs about the natural world, lost love, and the simple life on rancheros, or ranches.

Ranchera songs are played in several tempi, including slow waltzes in $3/4$ time, fast polkas in $2/4$ time, and boleros in $4/4$ time. Musicians play ranchera on guitars, horns, guitarrons, and accordions. In the 1940s, this style was popularized by José Alfredo Jiménez, who wrote and recorded over four hundred ranchera songs. Today, the most famous ranchera star is Juan Gabriel, born in Michoacán in 1950. He began singing and writing original ranchera songs at the age of thirteen. By the 1980s, Gabriel was an international star. He has sold over 30 million records throughout Latin America.

Unlike mariachi music, which is largely played by men, ranchera is popular with many of Mexico's most famous female singers, called divas. In the 1920s, Lucha Reyes was the first ranchera singer to achieve international fame, performing in several movies and playing in Mexico, Los Angeles, and Europe. In recent years,

Popular throughout Latin America, Juan Gabriel is synonymous with Mexican ranchera country music and has enjoyed a long career spanning three decades.

diva Astrid Hadad has stimulated renewed interest in Reyes's music by recording some of her classic songs.

Musical Newspapers

Ranchera is among many Mexican styles that arose in the rural countryside. The music of corrido also expresses the feelings of poor Mexican peasants. Rather than drawing upon sentimental and nostalgic feelings, however, corrido is a form of protest music meant to agitate and annoy government officials.

The widespread appreciation of corrido first came about between 1910 and 1920, when Mexico was undergoing a bloody political revolution against authoritarian government leaders. In this era, newspaper and radio content was strictly controlled by government and business. The only way for average people to voice their opinions about war, unemployment, the struggles against powerful landowners, and revolutionary heroes like Francisco "Pancho" Villa was through corrido lyrics. Because of their content, corridos were originally known as musical newspapers, but rather than relate straight news, the songs used commentary to interpret, celebrate, and honor the subjects of the song.

In its standard form, corrido contains long strings of quatrains, or four-line verses. At the beginning of the song, the singer gives a salutation and provides a prologue, or background, to the rest of the verses. The second part of the corrido tells a story of current events. The song often ends with a moral lesson and a farewell from the singer. Corrido singers, or corridistas, use straightforward delivery, unlike the emotional singing used in ranchera, so that the verses may be clearly understood by the listener. The musical accompaniment to the corrido is most often an accordion, guitar, and percussion instruments playing in $3/4$ time.

Glorifying Banditos

In the early days of corrido, revolutionaries such as Villa were honored as heroes even as authorities characterized them as outlaws and bandits. The tradition of glorifying banditos remains alive in modern corrido as some singers from northern Mexico, called norteño musicians, compose narco-corridos to celebrate the deeds of drug lords and narcotics traffickers. Although these songs are heavily criticized in the press and banned from the airwaves in Mexico, they are extremely popular among young Spanish-speaking audiences on both sides of the Mexican-U.S. border.

Los Tigres del Norte was one of the first bands to record best-selling narco-corrido songs. The band was formed in 1970 in Sinaloa, a state in northern Mexico, by accordionist Jorge Hernández, his two brothers Raul and Hernan, and their cousin Oscar Lara. When the group moved to San Jose, California, in the early 1970s, the police called them the Little Tigers, giving them part of their name. Their first hit, "Contrabando y Traicion" ("Contraband and Betrayal"), was recorded in 1972. During this era, before the advent of gangsta rap and hip-hop, the song, about drug traders, love, and betrayal, was extremely controversial. It became a major Latin hit, however, and the band achieved phenomenal success with other songs about drug runners and the travails of illegal immigrants.

Los Tigres del Norte continues to sell millions of records on both sides of the border, and the band has been credited with turning norteño music into an international genre. In 2005,

Members of the norteno group Los Tigres del Norte perform at the Latin Grammy Awards in 2005. The band is known for its narcocorridos.

the band celebrated its thirty-fifth anniversary in the music business, and their musical repertoire continues to grow. Los Tigres del Norte continually updates its musical sounds with elements of rock, cumbia, and attention-grabbing effects such as machine guns and sirens.

The Banda Boom

Not all norteño music is concerned with the deeds of outlaws, and the form has evolved into other styles in recent decades. For example, in the late 1960s, norteño groups began to hire musicians who played trumpets, trombones, saxophones, tubas, clarinets, and percussion instruments such as the tambora drum. What emerged was a new style called banda, in which six to twenty musicians play rancheras, corridos, cumbias, and boleros.

Banda music has exploded in popularity throughout Mexico, where it is a staple on radio and television. Concerts by groups such as Banda el

Corrido of the Mexican Revolutionary

The Mexican revolutionary hero Francisco "Pancho" Villa was assassinated by unknown assailants in 1923. Lyrics to the corrido excerpted below were composed only sixty days after the event. The song, "Corrido Historia y Muerte del Gral. Francisco Villa" ("Corrido History and Murder of General Francisco Villa"), was used to take the news of Villa's death to villagers throughout the Mexican countryside.

In a hacienda in my country,
marvelous México,
  from a worker of the land
  the great General Villa was
    born. . . .
  He joined Madero's forces
  with a strong hand,
  and the once lowly farm-
    worker
  became an undefeated rebel.
  Due to his extraordinary
    bravery
  and unsurpassed fierceness,

at Rellano Don Pancho
  (Madero)
promoted him to the rank
  of general. . . .
But envy and treachery
lurked nearby
waiting for the opportunity
to take his life.
Near Parral,
the motive has yet to be
  discovered,
they killed the General
as he was driving his
  automobile. . . .
His soldiers grieved for him
because he was their hope,
and the brave Dorados
swore to avenge his death. . . .
May you rest in peace,
  because your name
shines like a star in history:
immortal will be the fame
of General Pancho Villa.

"Corrido Historia y Muerte del Gral. Francisco Villa," Artsedge. http://artsedge.kennedy-center.org/content/3738/3738_mexRev_historia.pdf.

Recodo fill stadiums, while nearly every small village hosts a banda concert each weekend. The banda craze has also created new dance fads such as the quebradita, described as an acrobatic combination of the polka, lambada, cumbia, and jitterbug.

While banda remains the premier music style of Mexico, its status has been challenged in recent years by

Francisco "Pancho" Villa, one of the foremost leaders of the Mexican revolution, is shown here. Villa is the subject of countless corridos.

techno-banda, a modernized version of the sound featuring digital synthesizers, electric bass and guitar, and tooth-rattling sound systems. Techno-bandas are limited to seven or eight members but also feature vocalists, who play only minor roles in traditional banda.

Tex-Mex Border Music

Northern Mexico has been a source of musical creativity for many decades, and the banda boom is only the latest chapter in this tradition. In the United States, another tradition is at work as musicians have developed unique styles for fans along the Texas border. Tejano music, or Tex-Mex, is a style that was first played by bandleader Isidro Lopez when he added an accordion to his big band sound in the mid-1950s.

Lopez and other musicians formed the Tex-Mex style out of a combination of ranchera and corrido sounds. In later years, musicians added elements of norteño, rock, cumbia, American country, and blues. Traditionally, Tejano groups consist of five- or six-member combos with drums, bass, guitar, horns, and a lead accordion cranking out a one-two, one-two polka beat. As the music grew in popularity in the 1980s, the Tejano sound was updated with keyboards and synthesizers, and an electronic disco beat was added to the mix.

Mexican American Rock and Roll

Many Tex-Mex musicians remain true to their musical roots. However, there has been a long tradition of Latin musicians shaping American pop and rock and roll. For example, one of the biggest acts of late 1950s was the Mexican American Richard Valenzuela, known as Ritchie Valens. Although he was born in Los Angeles, Valens often traveled to Mexico, where he first heard the three-hundred-year-old folk song "La Bamba." Valens recorded the song with a rock tempo, an Afro-Cuban drum, and lyrics in Spanish. Although Valens did not speak the language and had to sing the lyrics phonetically, "La Bamba" became the first Spanish-language record to reach number one on the Billboard charts. After "La Bamba," Valens was set to become the biggest Mexican American rock star in history. His career was cut short after he had been on the national scene for only eight months, however, when a plane that was transporting him from a gig in Iowa crashed on February 3, 1959.

Richie Valens, the first Mexican American musician to cross over into mainstream American rock and roll, died in a plane crash at a young age.

The Latin influence on rock and roll did not die with Valens. For example, in the 1960s, a few Mexican American rock bands began using the electronic Farfisa organ instead of the accordion. The sound of the Farfisa is often described as "cheesy" by music critics. However, the organ had a distinctive sound that propelled rock-and-roll songs such as "96 Tears" by Mexican American rockers ? (Question Mark) and the Mysterians to number one. As Morales writes, the organ was more than a melody instrument in the hands of Mysterian Bobby Balderrama:

> 96 Tears uses the organ as a percussive instrument the way Afro-Cuban music does, building to an other-worldly, moody apotheosis [elevation], especially when combined with [Question Mark's] eerie vocals. The Mysterians' music seemed to announce that as Mexican-Americans, they felt like aliens.[40]

The band ? and the Mysterians was one among several Mexican American acts that produced classic songs that are still heard on oldies radio stations today. Cannibal and the Headhunters, from East Los Angeles, also became major stars for a brief time with their now-classic "Land of a Thousand Dances." Songwriters Chan Romero and Chris Montez wrote several hit songs, including "Hippy Hippy Shake," which was recorded by the Beatles and others. A band called the Champs had a huge hit with their song

"Tequila," which was on the charts for nineteen weeks in 1958. The saxophonist for the Champs, Chuck Rio, was a Latino musician from Texas whose lead melody, inspired by the Afro-Cuban style, helped the song win a Grammy in 1958. "Tequila" was popularized again in the 1980s by comedian Pee Wee Herman and is still played by countless bands today. Another Latino band, Sam the Sham and the Pharaohs, took the Tex-Mex sound national with songs such as "Wooly Bully." Writing about the Mexican American influence on classic rock, Morales states:

> The legacy laid down by Ritchie Valens and the Chicano rockers of the early 1960s was at the root of an entire branch of American rock history, one that many consider to be the most authentic "American" do-it-yourself style. . . . [Genres] popularized in the early to mid-'60s, such as frat rock, party rock, and garage rock, and possibly surf music, all sounds that immediately preceded or developed in tandem with the Beatles . . . were at least partly grounded in the hybrid Mexican-American cultures that had already absorbed Afro-Cuban music through Mexico's mambo period in the 1950s.[41]

The California Connection

The influence of Mexican Americans on rock did not stop in the mid-1960s. Carlos Santana, born in a small Mexi-can town near Guadalajara, grew up in Tijuana. After moving to San Francisco at fourteen, Santana formed his eponymous band to play rock with a strong Afro-Cuban beat. In 1969, Santana played the Woodstock Music and Arts Festival and became a major star overnight with songs such as "Black Magic Woman" and Tito Puente's "Oye Como Va."

Although the group he founded broke up after four albums, Santana continues to create music. In 1999, he collaborated with some of the decade's biggest artists on the album *Supernatural*. The first single from the album, "Smooth," was a salsa-based rocker. The song "Corazón Espinado" was a collaboration with the Mexican rock band Maná. The album, with its irresistible Latin rhythms, went on to sell 15 million copies and earn Santana several Grammys.

Los Lobos is another Grammy-winning band from California. The group has sold millions of albums by blending rock and roll, Tex-Mex, folk, rhythm and blues, and traditional Mexican boleros and corridos. Los Lobos made several critically acclaimed albums in the early 1980s, but their breakthrough came in 1987 when they recorded songs for the soundtrack of the movie *La Bamba*, about the life and death of Ritchie Valens. Their version of "La Bamba" became a number one single. The following year, Los Lobos got back to their roots with the album *La Pistola y el Corazón*, which featured both original and classic norteño songs. Although the album was not a best seller, Los Lobos became well known on the national circuit by working as an opening act for superstars such as Bob Dylan and the Grateful Dead.

In recent years, the band has continued to flourish as the nation's premier Mexican American rock act. By 2004, the band was celebrating nearly thirty years in the music business and the release of more than fifteen

Battle of the Bandas

As the digitized sound of techno-banda grew in popularity in the 1990s, it displaced established banda played the traditional style. The battle between banda and techno-banda is described by Helena Simonette in Banda: Mexican Musical Life Across Borders*:*

When technobanda hit Southern California in the early 1990s, there was no question among banderos [banda musicians] working in the Los Angeles area that this new musical trend would have a lasting impact on their own music, their repertory, as well as their economic situation. How it would affect their musical lives depended on the type of the banda (local, regional, or transnational), place of residence (Mexico or the United States), orientation (mass market or small-scale live performance), ambition, and other, individual,

factors. The clarinetist and bandleader Felipe Hernandez, who settled down in Los Angeles in the 1980s, summarized technobanda's influence on the local Sinaloan banda: "The technobanda movement did not help *banda sinaloense* at all. [The] only thing they accomplished was to ruin what we used to earn. They are six or seven musicians, we are a banda of fifteen. When I formed my banda, I charged $1,500–1,600 for two sets. Nowadays they pay me $800. Why? Because when [the technobandas] came out, it was what people liked. If they get $100 for each [musician], that's a good salary." Relying on synthesizer and electric instruments, technobanda was able to downsize its ensemble to half or a third of the personnel of an acoustic banda.

Helena Simonette, *Banda: Mexican Musical Life Across Borders*. Middletown, CT: Wesleyan University Press, 2001, pp. 263–64.

Carlos Santana's musical contributions cannot be underestimated. He has delighted audiences for decades with his unique blend of Afro-Cuban rhythms, salsa, and rock.

albums. Their DVD *Live at the Fillmore* shows them playing twenty-one songs in a variety of Latin styles, including Cuban jazz and even mariachi-influenced reggae.

From Tejano to International Stardom

Los Lobos has a loyal audience that appreciates their diversity rooted in rock. Few Mexican American artists, however, can match the success of Selena Quintanilla, known simply as Selena, a Tejano singer who rose to the top of the international pop charts in the 1990s.

Selena was a musical prodigy who began her performing career in her father's Mexican restaurant in Lake Jackson, Texas, in 1979. She recorded her first songs the next year at the age of nine. During her adolescent years, Selena spent most of her time playing Tejano music in concert venues in the Southwest. Like Ritchie Valens, Selena did not speak Spanish, but learned to sing her songs phonetically.

Selena was signed to Capital EMI Records in 1989. After releasing several albums, she became an international star in 1994 with the tremendously popular *Amor Prohibido*. The album sold so well that it knocked Gloria Estefan's smash hit *Mi Tierra* out of the number one spot on *Billboard*'s Latin music chart. The same year, Selena won a Grammy Award for best Mexican American album for her CD *Selena Live*.

One of Selena's many admirers, Yolanda Saldívar, became president of the Selena Fan Club. In 1995, however, it was discovered that Saldívar was embezzling money from the singer. Selena agreed to meet Saldívar at a hotel on March 31, 1995, in order to retrieve paperwork from her. The women got into an argument over the embezzled funds, and Saldívar shot Selena once in the back. Selena died several hours later from blood loss. Her tragic death shocked her fans. Vigils and memorials in her honor were held throughout Mexico and the United States, and her funeral drew sixty thousand mourners.

Selena's posthumously released album, *Dreaming of You*, debuted at number one on the *Billboard* music charts, making her the first Hispanic singer to accomplish this feat. On its release date, it sold over 175,000 copies, the most ever by any female singer in pop history. In 1997, Jennifer Lopez played Selena in the movie of the same name, and the role made her a major star.

Although Selena died tragically, she took Tejano from the Texas border to fans around the globe. As a sound that mixes many elements from the American melting pot, Tejano music has become a distinct regional sound with an international flavor.

A Universal Sound

Selena's music can still be heard on radio stations throughout the world, along with that of the latest Latina and Latino stars. In the twenty-first century, Mexican music has gone global with dozens

More than a decade after her death, Selena Quintanilla remains the definitive international icon of Tejano music.

of satellite, Internet, and cable radio stations dedicated to Latin rock, soul, rap, and hip-hop. Cable TV channels such as Music Choice offer programming such as Rock en Español, with cutting-edge sounds from Spanish-language rock artists including Maná, Control Machete, Kinky, Julieta Venegas, and Molotov. The Mexicana channel offers traditional styles with ranchera, banda, and mariachi artists such as Pepe Aguilar, Joan Sebastian, and Paquita La Del Barrio. There are also stations dedicated to salsa and merengue, urban sounds, and Latin pop.

Music that has been forged in a merging of Amerindian, African, and European cultures in the past four centuries has become a universal sound. Without the influence of Latin musicians, many musical forms throughout the world might never have evolved. As it stands, wherever there are congas, claves, guitars, and trumpets playing joyous dance beats, the sounds of the Mesoamericans from centuries past are still alive. Whether the music is salsa, son, mambo, samba, corrido, or Tejano, the Latin rhythms will never fade.

• Notes •

Introduction: A Global Beat

1. Quoted in Ed Morales, *The Latin Beat*. New York: Da Capo, 2003, p. xviii.
2. Morales, *The Latin Beat*, pp. xx–xxi.

Chapter One: Roots Music

3. Laurence E. Schmeckebier, *Modern Mexican Art*. Minneapolis: University of Minnesota Press, 1939, p. 4.
4. Quoted in Robert Stevenson, *Music in Aztec and Inca Territory*. Berkeley and Los Angeles: University of California Press, 1968, pp. 14–15.
5. Alba Herrera y Ogazon, *The Musical Art of Mexico*. Mexico City: Direccion General de las Bellas Artes, 1917, p. 9.
6. Richard Anderson, "Our Recordings," Folkways. www.folkways.si.edu/search/AlbumDetails.aspx?ID=800.
7. Robert Stevenson, *The Music of Peru*. Washington, DC: Pan American Union, 1960, p. 39.
8. Stevenson, *The Music of Peru*, p. 14.
9. Dale A. Olsen, "An Introduction to the Music and Culture of the Warao Indians of Venezuela," Dolsenmusic.com. www.dolsenmusic.com/advocacy/Warao/Warao%20Indians warao_indians_venezuela;202004.html, 2004.

10. John Storm Roberts, *Black Music of Two Worlds*. New York: Schirmer, 1998, p. xxiii.
11. Morales, *The Latin Beat*, pp. xiv–xv.
12. Morales, *The Latin Beat*, p. xv.

Chapter Two: Caribbean Spice

13. Quoted in Maya Roy, *Cuban Music*. Princeton, NJ: Markus Wiener, 2002, p. 8.
14. Roy, *Cuban Music*, p. 8.
15. Roy, *Cuban Music*, p. 18.
16. Isabelle Leymarie, *Cuban Fire*. London: Continuum, 2002, p. 24.
17. Quoted in Morales, *The Latin Beat*, p. 7.
18. Quoted in Vernon W. Boggs, *Salsiology*. New York: Excelsior Music, 1992, p. 99.
19. Boggs, *Salsiology*, p. 84.
20. Morales, *The Latin Beat*, p. 84.

Chapter Three: Brazilian Beats

21. Chris McGowan and Ricardo Pessanha, *Brazilian Sound*. New York: Billboard, 1991, p. 23.
22. Quoted in David Appleby, *The Music of Brazil*. Austin: University of Texas Press, 1983, p. 61.
23. McGowan and Pessanha, *Brazilian Sound*, pp. 29–30.
24. Quoted in McGowan and Pessanha, *Brazilian Sound*, p. 30.

25. Quoted in McGowan and Pessanha, *Brazilian Sound*, p. 38.
26. Quoted in Lisa Shaw, *A Social History of the Brazilian Samba*. Brookfield, VT: Ashgate, 1999, p. 7.
27. McGowan and Pessanha, *Brazilian Sound*, pp. 48–49.
28. Quoted in McGowan and Pessanha, *Brazilian Sound*, p. 68.
29. Christopher Dunn, *Brutality Garden*. Chapel Hill: University of North Carolina Press, 2001, p. 3.
30. Jan Field, "Boyz from Brazil—Brazilian Rap," Findarticles.com. www.findarticles.com/p/articles/mi_m0268/is_n8_v34/ai_18387596.

Chapter Four: Music of South America

31. Morales, *The Latin Beat*, p. 253.
32. Quoted in Roberts, *Black Music of Two Worlds*, p. 88.
33. Quoted in Sharna Fabian, "Tango Music," Worldhistory.com. www.world history.com/wiki/T/Tango-music.htm.

34. Quoted in Nicolas Slonimsky, *Music of Latin America*. New York: Da Capo, 1972, p. 61.
35. Quoted in Simon Broughton and Mark Ellingham, eds., *World Music: Latin and North America, Caribbean, India, Asia and Pacific*. London: Rough Guides, 2000, p. 363.
36. Quoted in Broughton and Ellingham, *World Music*, p. 366.
37. Quoted in Latin American Music, North Carolina State University. http://social.chass.ncsu.edu/slatta/hi216/music.htm.

Chapter Five: Mexican Music in Two Nations

38. Dale A. Olsen and Daniel E. Sheehy, eds., *The Garland Handbook of Latin American Music*. New York: Garland, 2000, p. 145.
39. Quoted in Broughton and Ellingham, *World Music*, pp. 466–67.
40. Morales, *The Latin Beat*, p. 290.
41. Morales, *The Latin Beat*, p. 288.

• For Further Reading •

Books

Bárbara Cruz, *Rubén Blades: Salsa Singer and Social Activist*. Springfield, NJ: Enslow, 1997. Traces the life of the international salsa singing star from his early life in Panama through his career as a musician and actor and his unsuccessful run for the presidency of his home country.

Leonardo Padura Fuentes, *Faces of Salsa: A Spoken History of the Music*. Washington, DC: Smithsonian, 2003. Interviews with some of the most famous creators of salsa, filled with personal revelations by the musicians, historical detail about their lives and times, and colorful anecdotes about their identities, friendships, and working relationships.

Nancy E. Krulik, *Pop Goes Latin*. New York: Grosset & Dunlap, 1999. An introduction to the contemporary Latin music scene with profiles of eleven acts, including Ricky Martin, Jennifer Lopez, Enrique Iglesias, and Marc Anthony.

Herón Marquez, *Latin Sensations*. Minneapolis: Lerner, 2001. Profiles five influential Latino entertainers of the 1990s—Ricky Martin, Selena, Jennifer Lopez, Enrique Iglesias, and Marc Anthony—details their rise to stardom and their influence on the American music scene.

Mary Olmstead, *Tito Puente*. Chicago: Raintree, 2005. A biography of the bandleader and recording artist who gained worldwide popularity as the King of Mambo.

Max Salazar, *Mambo Kingdom: Latin Music in New York*. New York: Schirmer, 2003. The story of Afro-Cuban, mambo, salsa, and Latin-jazz scenes in Manhattan, with profiles of Tito Puente, Machito, Tito Rodriguez, Charlie and Eddie Palmieri, and others.

Sue Steward, *Musica! Salsa, Rumba, Merengue, and More: The Rhythm of Latin America*. San Francisco: Chronicle, 1999. A comprehensive guide to salsa music, its history, and its biggest stars, with an introduction by salsa superstar Willie Colón.

Pablo Ellicott Yglesias, *Cocinando: Fifty Years of Latin Album Covers*. New York: Princeton Architectural Press, 2005. A visual history of salsa, rock, mambo, jazz, and other Latin styles depicted in the vivid color reproductions of album covers from the last fifty years.

Internet Sources

Jennifer Brozensky, Esperanza Cabrera, Kristi Collins, "Cuba and Its

Music," Cedar Crest College. www2.cedarcrest.edu/academic/soc/ccameron/soc215/cuba/cuba.htm.

Dale A. Olsen, "An Introduction to the Music and Culture of the Warao Indians of Venezuela," Dolsenmusic. com. www.dolsenmusic.com/advocacy/Warao/Warao;20Indians /warao_indians_venezuela%202 004.html.

Web Sites

Atlas of Plucked Instruments (www. atlasofpluckedinstruments.com). A Web site dedicated to common and unusual stringed instruments from around the world, with fascinating photos and musical histories of instruments ancient and modern from Latin America, India, Asia, and elsewhere.

Latin American Music, North Carolina State University. (http:// social.chass.ncsu.edu/slatta/hi216/ music.htm). Biographical information about and photos of important Latin music makers, details about the cultural and political impact of various musical styles, and links for further information.

The Mexican Folkloric Dance Co. of Chicago (www.mexfoldanco.org/ Thumbs.htm). Photographs of brightly costumed dancers performing traditional steps from sixteen distinct regions of Mexico, with links to descriptions of the musical styles associated with the dances.

• Index •

accordions, 44, 64, 66, 81, 82, 85
acid-jazz, 60
acid-rock, 70
Africa
 influences from, 10, 12–14, 21, 44, 45, 47,
  62–63, 92
 music of, 26–33, 58–59, 66, 76, 77–78
Afro-Brazilian music, 47, 51
Afro-Cuban music, 12, 38–43, 64, 86, 87
Afro-Spanish music, 24, 26–29, 40
Afro-X (rapper), 60
agogo (instrument), 49
Aguilar, Pepe, 92
Akan people, 26
Alcione (singer), 53–54
alegro drums, 63
Allende, Salvador, 73
Amazon, music of, 14, 21–23, 26, 62
Amerindians
 influences from, 10, 13–17, 47, 62–64,
  66, 92
 music of, 19, 21, 73, 76, 77–78
Amor Prohibido (album), 90
Andes, music of, 19, 23
Angola, influences from, 45, 47
antaras (instrument), 20–21
Anthony, Marc, 43–44
Arabs, influences from, 29
Argentina, music of, 12, 29, 62, 65–71, 75
Ashanti people, 45
atabaque drums, 49
Aztec people, influences from, 14–19, 29,
 77

back beats, 64
Baez, Joan, 73
Baker, Chet, 54
Balderrama, Bobby, 86
ballads, 10, 12, 29, 63–64
Banda el Recodo (group), 83–84
banda music, 77, 83–85, 88, 92
banditos, 82–83
bandoneons (instrument), 67
bands, 19–20, 31–32, 51, 63, 64

bandurrias (instrument), 30
Bantu people, 45, 66
barrios, music of, 40, 41–42
 see also slums
bass (instrument), 12, 40, 44, 61, 67, 85
bassoons, 18, 31
bata drums, 32
bataque music, 47, 49, 61
Bauza, Mario, 39
Beatles (group), 12, 55, 68, 86, 87
Beck (singer), 59
Benin, influences from, 30
Bethânia, Maria, 59
"Beto bom de bola" (song), 56
Bicycle (album), 70
big band music, 39, 64
"Bim-Bom" (song), 54
birth, songs for, 23
"Black Magic Woman" (song), 87
blacks, 12, 26, 32, 35, 45, 62
Blades, Rubén, 43
blues music, 12, 85
bolero music, 29, 81, 83, 87
Bolivia, music of, 19, 21, 62, 64
bombo drums, 20–21, 63
bongo drums, 37, 40
Bosco, João, 59
bossa nova, 45, 54–55, 58, 60, 62
Branco, Humberto Castelo, 56, 57
Brazil, music of, 43, 44, 45–61
Bridge over Troubled Water (album), 21
Browne, Jackson, 76
Buarque, Chico, 57
Buena Vista Social Club (album/film), 38
Buenos Aires (Argentina), 65–68, 75
Byrd, Charlie, 54
Byrne, David, 34, 59

cabildos (societies), 33
cajóns (instrument), 35
California, 12, 77, 87–89, 91
call-and-response singing, 27, 36, 47, 49
Cameroon, influences from, 30
Canary Islands, influences from, 29, 30

Cannibal and the Headhunters (group), 86
Caribbean, music of, 12, 30–44, 66
Carnaval, 45, 50–54
Carvalho, Beth, 53, 54
cavaquinho (instrument), 50, 53
celebration music, 62–64, 79
Central America, 14, 77
ceremonies, music for, 16–17, 19, 26, 31–32
cha-cha-cha, 39, 41, 64
Champs (group), 86–87
charangos (instrument), 21
Chau (album), 75
"Chega de Saudade" (song), 54
Chiapas (Mexico), 19
Chile, music of, 62, 64, 70–74, 76
"Chile Stadium" (poem), 73–74
church music, 18, 31–32
clapping, 47, 48, 50
clarinets, 31, 40, 63, 83
classical music, 32
claves (instrument), 36, 40, 43, 92
Cobain, Kurt, 59
Colombia, music of, 12, 29, 43, 44, 62–65
Colón, Willie, 42–43
columbia (dance), 36
communication
    long-distance, 19
    supernatural, 14, 23–24, 32–33
competitions, Brazilian, 56–58, 79
conch shells, 16–17, 19
conga drums, 36, 39, 40, 92
Congo, influences from, 30, 44, 45
conjunto music, 12
conquistadores, 15–16
"Contrabando y Traicion" (song), 82
Control Machete (group), 92
Cooder, Ry, 38
"Cool Mulatto" (song), 51
"Corazón Espinado" (song), 87
cornetts, 18
"Corrido Historia y Muerte del Gral. Francisco Villa" (song), 84
corrido music, 12, 29, 81–82, 83, 85, 87, 92
Cortés, Hernán, 15
Costa, Gal, 59
country songs, 66, 81, 85
cowbells, 40
"Crazy Boots" (song), 70
Creole people, 31–32
Cruz, Celia, 34, 43
Cuba, music of, 10, 12, 29, 30–44, 48, 66, 78

Cuban Fire (film), 35
Cuban Love Song (film), 38
Cugat, Xavier, 38
cuica drums, 49
cumbia music, 62–65, 83, 84, 85
current events songs, 36, 80, 82, 84

dakotutuma, 21
dancing
    group, 14, 30
    music for, 12, 26, 31–32, 44, 49, 80, 92
    ritual, 15, 19, 24, 35, 47
    see also individual dances
Dark Latin Groove (group), 44
death, songs for, 23
decima songs, 29, 36
Dexter (rapper), 60
Díaz, Bernal, 16
digital music, 43, 65, 68, 85, 88
Dinamita, La Sonora (singer), 64
Disco Fuentes (record label), 64
disco music, 43, 85
divas, 81
D-Lita, Pedro (rapper), 60
Dominican Republic, music of, 40, 44
Domino, Fats, 12
Downs, Lila, 79
Dreaming of You (album), 90
drug songs, 61, 82
drumming/drums, 18, 31–36, 65, 85
    African, 12, 26–29, 30, 44, 47, 51, 63
    Brazilian, 50, 53, 61
    indigenous, 16, 19–21
Dylan, Bob, 12, 88

Ecuador, music of, 19, 21, 62, 64
Egypt, influences from, 30
ehuru drums, 24
"El Cóndor Pasa" (song), 21
electronic music, 12, 44, 86, 88
El Gallo (singer), 36
El Salvador, music of, 64
"Enchale Salsita" (song), 40
England, influences from, 30, 59
Estefan, Gloria, 43–44, 90
Europe
    influences from, 12–14, 21, 30–31, 51, 62, 66, 92
    music of, 10, 17–19, 29, 47, 76–77
    tango in, 68
Ewe people, 45

fado music, 58
fandango music, 47
Fania (record label), 42–43
Fania All Stars (group), 43
Farfisa organs, 12, 86
Fattiqueira (singer), 61
fertility songs, 23, 47
fifes, 31
Firpo, Roberto, 68
five-beat rhythm, 12
"509-E" (song), 60
flamenco music, 66
flutes, 31, 67
    cane, 63, 73
    indigenous, 16, 18, 19, 21, 24, 28
    making of, 26
folk music, 21, 29, 42, 58, 60, 71, 77,
    87
Fon people, 45
foot-stamp dancing, 78
"Forbidding is Forbidden" (song), 58
France, influences from, 29, 30, 48
frevo music, 59
Fruko (bandleader), 64
funk music, 40, 59, 60, 70
Furtado, Nelly, 59
fusilamento style, 44

Gabriel, Juan, 81
Gabriel, Peter, 76
gaita (instrument), 63–64
Garcia, Charly, 68, 70
Gardél, Carlos, 68, 69
Germany, influences from, 10
    see also polkas
Getz, Stan, 54
Getz/Gilberto (album), 54
Ghana, influences from, 26, 30, 45
Gil, Gilberto, 58–60
Gilberto, Astrud, 54
Gilberto, João, 54
Gillespie, Dizzy, 39
"Girl from Ipanema, The" (song), 54
Grateful Dead, 88
Grillo, Frank Raul, 39
guaguanco (dance), 36
Guajiro people, 24
Guatemala, 19
Guinea, influences from, 62, 64
Güiraldes, Ricardo, 67–68
guiros (instrument), 30, 44

guitarrons (instrument), 79, 81
guitars, 19, 21, 28, 67
    Brazilian, 50, 53, 54
    Caribbean, 40, 44
    electric, 58, 85
    Mexican, 79, 80, 81, 82, 92
    Spanish, 18, 30, 63
Guthrie, Woody, 12
gypsy music, 29

habanera (dance), 12, 48, 66
Hadad, Astrid, 81
haravi (songs), 23
Harguindeguy, Eduardo, 70
harmonies, 10, 14, 47, 49, 54–55
harps, 18, 77, 79, 80
Harry, Debbie, 75
harvesting, songs for, 23
Hausa people, 45
healing, songs for, 23–24
heavy metal music, 60
Herman, Pee Wee, 87
Hernández, Antonio Valle, 32
Hernandez, Felipe, 88
Hernández, Hernan, 82
Hernández, Jorge, 82
Hernández, Raul, 82
hip-hop music, 12, 44, 60, 77
"Hippy Hippy Shake" (song), 86
Hola (album), 75
Holly, Buddy, 12
Honduras, 19
horns, 16, 30, 65, 77, 81, 85
horses, dancing, 80
huapanguera (instrument), 79
huehuetl (drums), 17
Huichilobos (Aztec god), 16
hunting, songs for, 23
hymns, 31

Iberian Peninsula, 27, 29
    see also Portugal, influences from;
        Spain
immigrant songs, 82
Inca people, music of, 14, 19–21, 23, 29
India, influences from, 14, 29
indigenous people, music of, 10, 14–29, 45,
    53, 62, 77
instruments
    African, 27–28, 33, 47
    electric, 58, 85, 88

European, 17–19, 63–64
indigenous, 14, 16–17, 19, 73
see also specific instruments
isimoi (instrument), 24
Isley Brothers (group), 12
Italy, influences from, 66
itotele drums, 32
Ivan y sus Bam Band (group), 65
iya drums, 32

jaguars, songs about, 22–23
Jamaica, music of, 12
Jara, Victor, 73–74
jarana (instrument), 79
jazz music, 10, 12, 64, 68
    Afro-Cuban, 39–40, 44, 90
    bebop, 54–55
Jiménez, José Alfredo, 81
jitterbug (dance), 84
Johnny MC (rapper), 60
"John Repression" (song), 70
John the Baptist, feast of, 64, 66
Jones, Mick, 75
juju music, 59

keyboards, 85
Kinky (group), 92

La Bamba (film), 87
"La Bamba" (song), 85–86, 87
lambada (dance), 84
"Land of a Thousand Dances" (song), 86
languages, 10, 26
Lara, Oscar, 82
Latin America, 10–14
Latin Tinge music, 10, 12
lauds (instrument), 28, 30
LaVoe, Héctor, 43
Leão, Lyra, 54
Lecuona, Ernesto, 38
Lee, Rita, 60
lemanjá (goddess), 47
Little Anecdotes About the Institutions
    (album), 70
Live at the Fillmore (DVD), 90
llamador drums, 63
looping, 61
Lopez, Isidro, 85
Lopez, Jennifer, 90
Los Beatniks (group), 68
Los Fabulosos Cadillacs (group), 70, 75

Los Lobos (group), 87–88, 90
Los Shakers (group), 68
Los Tigres del Norte (group), 82–83
love songs, 23, 43, 79, 80, 81
lucidez, 56
lullabies, 21–23, 26
lundu (dance), 47–48
lutes (instrument), 28, 73
lyrics, 14, 29, 36, 49, 55, 64, 79

Machito (group), 39–40
macumba (religion), 47, 53
magic, music for, 14
"Make Way" (song), 51
malandra/o, 51, 52
malembe music, 66
Mambo Aces (group), 40
mambo music, 10, 12, 39–40, 64, 87, 92
Maná (group), 87, 92
Manfugas, Nené, 36–37
manguebeat movement, 60
Mann, Herbie, 54–55
maracas (instrument), 30, 37
Marcha del Golazo Solitario (album), 75
marcha music, 49–50
mariachi music, 77, 79–81, 90, 92
Mariachi Vargas (group), 80
marimbula (instrument), 44
martial music, 14, 77
"Matador" (song), 75
maxixe music, 48–50
Maya people, influences from, 14, 19, 77
mazurkas (dance), 66
"Meeting with the Devil" (song), 70
Mendes, Sérgio, 54
merengue music, 40, 44, 64, 92
Mesoamericans, 21, 26, 77, 92
mestizo people, 77
Mexican-American music, 12, 77, 82, 85,
    86–87, 90
Mexican hat dance, 78
Mexico, music of, 10, 12, 14, 16–17, 19,
    29, 64, 77–92
Miami, Florida, 34, 43
Miami Sound Machine (group), 43
Middle East, influences from, 14, 28
military music, 49, 51
mina drums, 66
Mississippi Delta, music from, 12
Mi Tierra (album), 90
mixed-race people, 32

Modern Mayan: The Indian Music of Chiapas, Mexico (album), 19
Molotov (group), 92
Monarquia Indiana (Torquemada), 18
Montez, Chris, 86
Moors, influences from, 27–29
Morton, Jelly Roll, 12
motets (songs), 31
Mozárabic (language), 29
muhusemoi (instrument), 26
mulatto people, 32
Mulligan, Gerry, 54
Música Popular Brasileira (MPB), 55–58, 61
Mutations (album), 59

narcorrido music, 82
Nascimento, Milton, 59
Native Americans, influences from, 77
New Orleans, Louisiana, 10, 12
New York City, New York, 12, 34, 38–42, 40, 44, 64, 68
Nigeria, influences from, 30, 45
"96 Tears" (song), 86
norteno music, 77, 82–83, 85, 88
North Africa, influences from, 14, 27–29
Not Fade Away (album), 12
nueva cancion (songs), 29, 71–74, 76
Nunes, Clara, 53, 54

oboes, 18, 31
ocarinas (instrument), 19
"O Encanto do Gantois," 53
okonkolo drums, 32
olubatá (drummers), 33
"On the Phone" (song), 50
organs, 12, 17, 18, 31, 86
Orinoco Delta, music from, 21–23, 26
orishas (gods), 32, 33
Os Racionais MCs (group), 61
ouds (instrument), 63
"Oye Como Va" (song), 87

Pacheco, Maurício (rapper), 60
Paez, Fito, 70
pagode music, 53
Pais, João Pedro (singer), 61
Palladium Ballroom, 39–40
Panama, music of, 43, 64
pandeiro (instrument), 53
pandero drums, 79
panpipes, 20–21

Paquita La Del Barrio (group), 92
Paraguay, music of, 62
Parra, Violeta, 72–73
parranderos (singers), 64
payadores (songs), 73
peasants, 81
Peña de los Parra (club), 73
percussion instruments, 27, 30, 34–36, 49–50, 53, 82, 83, 86
    see also drumming/drums
Peru, music of, 10, 19–21
pianos, 40, 44, 47, 67
Piazolla, Astor, 68
Piñeiro, Ignacio, 40
Pinochet, Augusto, 73–74, 76
Pistola y el Corazón, La (album), 87–88
play, music for, 24
pleasure music, 14
plena music, 40
poetry, 14, 15, 73
political songs, 36, 61, 70–73
polkas, 10, 48, 66, 77, 81, 84, 85
polyrhythms, 36, 47, 68
Poma de Ayala, Huamán, 23
poncho bands, 21
pop music, 10, 12–13, 32, 43, 60, 85, 92
Portugal, influences from, 27, 45, 47, 58
PosseMente Zulu (group), 60
protest songs, 55–58, 60–61, 70–74, 76, 79, 81
psychedelic music, 12
Public Enemy (group), 61
Puente, Tito, 40, 87
Puerto Rico, music of, 12, 29, 34, 40–44, 64
punishment, music for, 26
punk music, 60

quatrains, 36, 82
quebradita (dance), 84
Quechua people, 21
Queen (group), 60
quenas (instrument), 21, 73
? (Question Mark) and the Mysterians (group), 86

rain forests, music of, 14, 21–23, 26, 62
ranchera songs, 81, 82, 83, 85, 92
rap music, 44, 60–61, 75
Rappin' Hood (rapper), 60
rasps (instrument), 17, 19
rattles, 17, 19, 24, 27–28, 30, 36, 44
rebecs, 18

redondo music, 66
reggae music, 12, 44, 59, 60, 64, 70, 75, 90
religious music, 14, 16, 24, 31–34, 47
repicador (instrument), 35
requinto (instrument), 79
revolutionary songs, 70–73, 80, 81–82, 84
Rey Azucar (album), 75
Reyes, Lucha, 81
rhythm and blues music, 87
rhythms, 10, 61, 65, 66, 68
    African, 12, 14, 27, 29, 64, 77–78
    dance, 43, 44, 80, 92
    rock, 12, 64
    see also polyrhythms
Ricardo, Sergio, 56
Rio, Chuck, 87
Rio de Janeiro (Brazil), 48–49
rituals, music for, 14, 15–16, 19, 32–34
rockabilly music, 12
rock-and-roll music, 10, 12, 40, 43–44, 65, 68,
    75
    Brazilian, 55, 58–59
    Mexican, 77, 83, 85–88, 90
Rock in Rio festival, 60–61
Rodriguez, Lalo, 43
Rodriguez, Tito, 40
Rogers, Shorty, 54
Roman Catholicism, 32, 47
Romero, Chan, 86
roots music, 10, 14–29, 45, 53, 62, 77
Rosa, Noel, 51
Rumba (film), 38
rumba music, 10, 34–36, 40
Run-DMC (group), 61

sackbuts (instrument), 18
Saldívar, Yolanda, 90
salidor (instrument), 35
salsa music, 10, 40–44, 64, 92
samba music, 10, 12, 44–45, 47, 49–55,
    58–62, 64, 75, 92
sampling, 44, 61
Sam the Sham and the Pharaohs (group), 87
Santamaria, Mongo, 34
Santana, Carlos, 87
Santeria (religion), 32–34
"Saudades Mil" (song), 60
saxophones, 40, 63, 83
scales, musical, 14, 21, 47
Science, Chico (rapper), 60
scrapers (instrument), 30, 63

Sebastian, Joan, 92
secular music, 31
Seeger, Pete, 76
seis songs, 29
sekeseke (instrument), 24
Selena (singer), 90
Senegal, influences from, 30
Serú Girán (group), 70
sewei (rattle), 24
Sexteto Habenero (group), 37
shamans, 24
"Shantytown Samba" (song), 52
Siembra (album), 43
Simon and Garfunkle (group), 21
singing, 14, 27, 30, 35–36, 47
ska music, 70, 75
slaves, 26, 30–33, 45, 47, 51, 62–65
slums, 48–49, 51, 65, 73
"Smooth" (song), 87
Sobrevivendo no Inferno (album), 61
sociedades, 51
Soda Stereo (group), 70
Somos Nós A Justica (group), 60
"Song for My Death" (song), 70
"Song of Alice in (Wonder) Land" (song), 70
songs, 14, 21, 28, 69
    see also ballads; *and specific titles and
        types of songs*
son music, 36–40, 78–80, 92
soukous music, 12
soul music, 40, 43, 44, 60
"Sou Negrão" (song), 60
South America, music of, 12, 14, 24, 62–76
Spain
    conquests by, 15–16, 23, 30, 62, 77
    influences from, 10, 12, 21, 27, 30–32,
        62–63, 66
    music of, 14, 17–19, 29, 47, 77–78
Spears, Britney, 61
spinets (instrument), 18
Springsteen, Bruce, 76
Stereo Maracañ (group), 60
Sting, 76
stride piano music, 12
stringed instruments, 27–28, 49
    see also specific instruments
Sudan, influences from, 45
Sui Generis (group), 68, 70
Supernatural (album), 87
surf music, 87
swing music, 39

synthesizers, 85, 88

Taino people, 30
tambora drums, 44, 63, 64, 83
tamborim (instrument), 53
tambourines, 16, 79
tango, 10, 12, 48, 65–68, 69, 71
Tango on Broadway, The (film), 69
techno-banda music, 77, 85, 88
techno-cumbia music, 65
techno music, 44
Tejano music, 77, 85, 90, 92
teponaztli (drums), 17
"Tequila" (song), 87
Tex-Mex border music, 12, 77, 82, 85, 86–87, 90
"Thanks to Life" (song), 73
theurgy songs, 23–24
thumb piano, 44
timbales (drums), 40
tom-toms, 40
toque music, 32
Torquemada, Juan de, 18
trap drums, 40
traveling, songs for, 26
trebles (instrument), 18
tres (instrument), 37
tres-dos (instrument), 35
trombones, 18, 43, 63, 83
tropicalia music, 57–60, 61
troubadours, 29, 79
trova songs, 29
Trujillo, Rafael, 44
trumpets, 37, 40, 64, 79, 83, 92
    Spanish, 16, 17, 18, 19, 31
tubas, 83
tumbador (instrument), 35
Twist and Shout (album), 12

United States
    influences from, 10, 12–13, 59
    tango in, 68
    see also Tex-Mex border music
urban music, 77, 92
Uruguay, music of, 62

Valens, Ritchie, 85–86, 87
Valentino, Rudolph, 12, 68
vallenato music, 29
Vandré, Geraldo, 57
Vargas, Wilfrido "El Barbarazo", 44
Vargas de Tecalitlán (group), 80
Vasos Vacios (album), 75
Veloso, Caetano, 58–59
"Ven, Devórame Otra Vez" (song), 43
Venegas, Julieta (singer), 92
Venezuela, music of, 12, 21, 26, 44, 62, 64, 66
vibrato, 29
Vida (album), 68
vihuela (instrument), 79
Villa, Francisco "Pancho," 82, 84
Viola, Paulinho da, 53
violas (instrument), 47–48
violins, 17, 24, 28, 31, 67, 79, 80
viols (instrument), 18, 31
vocal trill music, 29

Wai-Wai people, 24
waltzes, 79, 81
wandoras (instrument), 24
Warao people, 21–24, 26
war music, 16, 19, 23
wedding music, 19, 79
whistles, 16
"Who Am I Singing For, Then?" (song), 70
Winter, Paul, 54
woodwinds, 24, 27, 30, 49
    see also flutes
"Wooly Bully" (song), 87
work, songs for, 14, 21, 23, 24
working-class music, 34–35, 40, 51, 60, 62, 71

Xango (god), 47

yambu (dance), 36
Yaracuy (Venezuela), 66
Yekuana people, 24
Yoruba people, 30, 32–34, 45

zapateado (dance), 78–79
Zapotec Indians, 79

• Picture Credits •

Cover: © AFP/Getty Images
© AFP/Getty Images, 46, 53, 58
© Arlene Richie/Media Source/
    Getty Images, 91
© Bettmann/CORBIS, 15, 42, 55, 59,
    65, 69
© Bruno Domingos/Reuters/CORBIS,
    49
© Contagrapher ®/CORBIS, 81
© Daniel Laine/CORBIS, 37
© Ed George/Getty Images, 25
© Frank Driggs Collection/Getty
    Images, 41
© Frank Micelota/Getty Images, 89
© Free Agents Limited/CORBIS, 17
© Herve Collart/Sygma/CORBIS,
    22
© Hugh Sitton/zefa/CORBIS, 67

© Hulton-Archive/Getty Images, 38,
    86
© Hulton-Deutsch Collection/CORBIS,
    85
© Jose Azel/Aurora/Getty Images, 34
Maury Aaseng, 11
© Mike Blake/Reuters/CORBIS, 83
© Owen Franken/CORBIS, 63
© Reuters/CORBIS, 71, 72, 74
© Royalty-Free/CORBIS, 31
© S. Javelberg/Abril/zefa/CORBIS,
    50
© Sergio Durantes/CORBIS, 78
© Stapleton Collection/CORBIS, 28
© Staton R. Winter/Getty Images, 39
© Stephanie Maze/CORBIS, 48
© Werner Foreman/CORBIS, 18, 27
© Wolfgang Kaehler/CORBIS, 20

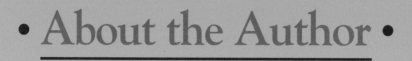

• About the Author •

Stuart A. Kallen is the author of more than two hundred nonfiction books for children and young adults. He has written on topics ranging from the theory of relativity to the history of rock and roll. In addition, Mr. Kallen has written award-winning children's videos and television scripts. In his spare time, Stuart A. Kallen is a singer/songwriter/guitarist in San Diego, California.